Cambridge |

Elements in Public and No
edited
Andrew Whitford
University of Georgia
Robert Christensen
Brigham Young University

THE HIDDEN TIER OF SOCIAL SERVICES

Frontline Workers' Provision of Informal Resources in the Public, Nonprofit, and Private Sectors

Einat Lavee
University of Haifa

CAMBRIDGE
UNIVERSITY PRESS

CAMBRIDGE
UNIVERSITY PRESS

University Printing House, Cambridge CB2 8BS, United Kingdom

One Liberty Plaza, 20th Floor, New York, NY 10006, USA

477 Williamstown Road, Port Melbourne, VIC 3207, Australia

314–321, 3rd Floor, Plot 3, Splendor Forum, Jasola District Centre, New Delhi – 110025, India

103 Penang Road, #05–06/07, Visioncrest Commercial, Singapore 238467

Cambridge University Press is part of the University of Cambridge.

It furthers the University's mission by disseminating knowledge in the pursuit of education, learning, and research at the highest international levels of excellence.

www.cambridge.org
Information on this title: www.cambridge.org/9781009101370
DOI: 10.1017/9781009105828

First published 2022

A catalogue record for this publication is available from the British Library.

ISBN 978-1-009-10137-0 Paperback
ISSN 2515-4303 (online)
ISSN 2515-429X (print)

The Hidden Tier of Social Services

Frontline Workers' Provision of Informal Resources in the Public, Nonprofit, and Private Sectors

Elements in Public and Nonprofit Administration

DOI: 10.1017/9781009105828
First published online: August 2022

Einat Lavee
University of Haifa

Author for correspondence: Einat Lavee, elavee@univ.haifa.ac.il

Abstract: What do frontline social service providers do during client interactions when they lack adequate formal organizational resources to respond to clients' needs? To answer this question, this Element presents two large-scale qualitative studies of Israeli frontline providers of social services. Drawing on interviews of public-sector workers (Study 1, N = 214), it introduces a widespread phenomenon, where the vast majority of frontline workers regularly provide a wide range of informal personal resources (IFRs) to clients. Study 2 (N = 84) then compares IFR provision between workers from the public, nonprofit, and private sectors. The comparative analysis demonstrates how workers' rationale for providing personal resources to clients is shaped by particular role perceptions embedded in values, norms, and behavioral expectations that vary by employment sector. The Element concludes by presenting ramifications of the phenomenon of IFR provision in terms of citizens' well-being, social inequality, gender relations, and the future of work in public administration.

Keywords: public services, informal resources, hybrid, frontline, discretion

ISBNs: 9781009101370 (PB), 9781009105828 (OC)
ISSNs: 2515-4303 (online), 2515-429X (print)

Contents

1 Introduction

This Element addresses a hidden tier of public services: informal practices of frontline workers, with particular attention to the personal resources the workers provide to their clients. These are resources that go above and beyond formal role requirements and are given at the expense of the workers' own capital. Such practices are enacted within the contemporary changing environment in public administration, in which workers are developing new coping strategies.

Comprehensive literature has described how workers adapt as they deliver services and provide *formal* resources (Brodkin, 2011; Evans & Hupe, 2020; Gofen, 2013; Thomann, van Engen & Tummers, 2018; Tummers et al., 2015; Zacka, 2018). Alongside these important studies, there are some hints in the literature that workers also respond to the changing environment by diverging from formal role expectations and providing clients with *personal* resources (Tummers et al., 2015), particularly when they lack adequate formal organizational resources (Dubois, 2016; Eldor, 2017).

This preliminary evidence has been the impetus of my own research. I have long felt that there is an entire hidden phenomenon alongside formal service provision, not yet fully explored or conceptualized. To establish the foundation of this Element, I devote its introduction to three cornerstones upon which I have built research exploring the hidden provision of informal personal resources by frontline workers to clients.

The first cornerstone draws on the research of organizational sociologist Mario Small, which focuses on organizations as resource providers. In the context of the post–welfare reform era in the United States, Small (2006) examined relations between organizations located in low-income neighborhoods (defining them as "neighborhood institutions") and the residents receiving services from these organizations. He argued that it is particularly important to explore mechanisms of resource provision from organizations to clients in times of welfare reform and reduced governmental resources. Small came to the conclusion that organizations operate as "resource brokers," linking their clients to external organizations with resources. In his case study of childcare centers, he showed how parents (i.e., clients of the organizations) received a wide range of resources provided by external organizations and brokered by the childcare centers. To name but a few of these resources, they included health-related information and low-cost or free medical examinations and treatments; legal information and advocacy; domestic abuse counseling; substance abuse treatment and counseling; adult language studies and work training; free access to museums, zoos, and other events; and free toys for Christmas (see Small, 2006, for further reading). Alluding to William Wilson's book, *The Truly Disadvantaged*, Small concluded that the truly disadvantaged are those who do not participate in organizations and thus lack access to the resources these organizations broker. What I have learned from Small's study is that organizations and their workers operate in varied ways, not always in keeping with their formal role definitions, and may provide resources beyond the formal organizational ones. These informal resources (IFRs) have the capacity to reduce inequality and enhance clients' well-being.

The other two cornerstones of this Element draw on studies I have conducted with colleagues, focusing on street-level workers who provide public social services in Israel. In the first set of studies, we examined what street-level workers do when they believe policy as designed might be harmful to their clients. We found that when workers believe there is a gap between designed policy and desirable policy, they engage in a variety of practices in an attempt to influence policy design (Lavee, Cohen & Nouman, 2018). For example, social workers who perceived urban renewal policy as severely detrimental to their low-income clients engaged in policy entrepreneurial practices, struggling to influence policy design (and succeeding). This required each of them to gain knowledge beyond their professional expertise, such as in planning, architecture, and engineering (Lavee & Cohen, 2019). From these studies, I learned that street-level workers take it upon themselves to "fix" inadequate policy in ways that go beyond their formal role, with the aim of protecting their clients and reducing inequality.

In the second set of studies, we examined practices of frontline service provision in welfare offices (Lavee & Strier, 2018, 2019) with the aim of understanding how welfare reform in Israel – where basic elements are similar to the neoliberal American reform – might be influencing the implementation work of social workers. Similar to Small's (2006) study, the larger context of our research was a reduction in formal governmental resources alongside increasing poverty rates. Focusing on discretionary practices during interactions with clients, we found that workers employ informal practices. In the absence of formal resources, they transfer emotional resources to clients. These emotional resources serve as a kind of capital that substitutes for the traditional social benefits that welfare services once provided to clients. From these studies I learned that, in an attempt to enhance clients' well-being, frontline social service providers struggle to implement policy, even partially, despite the absence of organizational resources. More specifically, I learned that, in the backdrop of scarce (formal) organizational material resources, workers provide informal personal-emotional alternative resources.

My main conclusion from the theoretical development in the field of organization–client relations and my own experience with studies of frontline providers of social services is that there is a hidden and unexplored tier of IFR provision. Contemporary cumulative knowledge on discretion and coping practices within the implementation work of frontline service providers has focused almost entirely on decisions made about the allocation of formal resources (i.e., those provided by the organization). Yet, clearly, alongside the provision of formal resources, another layer of service provision is taking place where informal, hidden practices are routinely enacted, and that layer has mostly remained beneath the surface, receiving little scholarly attention. In this Element, I address this lacuna by exploring discretionary practices and decisions made in the provision of informal personal resources, with the aim of uncovering the nature and extent of resources provided by frontline workers that are not part of their formal duties, or formal resources provided in informal ways (after hours, off duty).

Why is it that this phenomenon – something both practitioners and scholars are aware of – has not yet been explored in depth? I believe there are two complementary answers to this puzzle. First, like other silenced phenomena, unsilencing might lead to some undesirable results for those who are comfortable maintaining the status quo. Highlighting the informal personal services and resources that workers have to provide in their encounters with clients, in a context of scarce formal organizational resources, might raise new questions regarding the mismatch between demands and responses. Second, the lack of a comprehensive exploration of the provision of personal resources might be linked to methodological difficulties in exploring hidden practices and discretionary decisions.

In light of these challenges, I have made considerable effort to provide a solid conceptualization for this elusive phenomenon. I have thus drawn on the qualitative method, which is more suitable for exploring "under-the-surface" phenomena than surveys and questionnaires (Charmaz, 2014). With the help of trained research assistants, I have conducted two large-scale studies of frontline workers in Israel. The first entailed 214 in-depth interviews of public-sector frontline workers from three occupational areas: welfare, health, and education. The second study complemented the first by comparing public, nonprofit, and private sectors in terms of IFR provision, as welfare-state restructuring in Israel (similar to many other countries) has led to the parallel provision of social services by nonprofit and private organizations. This latter study included 83 in-depth interviews of frontline workers in the three employment sectors providing services in the same three domains (welfare, health, and education).

The findings presented in this Element contribute to the literature by exposing one more layer in the necessary, yet often unrecognized, component of informal service provision and by explaining how workers manage to implement policy and provide service to clients/citizens even in times of reduced formal resources. The study findings stress the fundamental role of frontline workers as mediators between designed policy and citizens' actual needs. Moreover, the comparative study of IFR provision between public, nonprofit and private sectors is essential in an era when the convergence of welfare reforms and New Public Management (NPM) imperatives has changed the nature of the provision of public services and has led to privatization of many public service areas.

The Element is structured in six sections. Section 2 provides a theoretical background, drawing on existing literature on discretion and coping strategies at the front line of public administration. The section places frontline practices in the context of welfare reforms and NPM imperatives, with a renewed focus on public value governance approaches. To set the frame for exploring informal service provision, this theoretical section concludes by presenting a few hints in contemporary literature of workers' provision of their personal resources.

Section 3 presents the general methodological design of the two qualitative studies. Study 1 was conducted with frontline workers in the public sector. Study 2 was conducted with frontline workers in the public, nonprofit, and private sectors.

The following two sections present the findings of these two studies. Section 4 establishes the existence of a phenomenon in which the vast majority of workers provide informal services and resources to their clients. The section also offers examples of the various types of IFRs provided. Section 5 then expands on the aspect of contemporary hybridity in the delivery of public services, establishing the rationale for sector comparison. It introduces the key finding of particular role perceptions, which constitute the rationale for the provision of IFRs in each sector. The section demonstrates how particular role perceptions shape the scope and content of IFR provision in the public, nonprofit, and private sectors.

Section 6 discusses an important aspect of IFR provision: its cost to frontline workers. This section empirically analyzes similarities and differences between sectors in terms of workers' perceptions of costs related to their informal practices. Findings underscore the key aspect of choice versus control over costs, which constitutes the main difference between workers from different sectors.

The Element concludes, in Section 7, by discussing several issues related to the provision of IFRs. These include its influence on clients'/citizens' well-being and social inequality; ramifications for public administration in general, particularly in terms of manpower renewal in the constrained environment of public-sector frontline workers; and gender ramifications, as the vast majority of social service workers are women. I close the section by suggesting that the knowledge yielded from a nuanced conceptualization of the IFR phenomenon might inform more adequate future policy, proposing several policy examples.

2 Discretion on the Front Line in Context

Frontline workers' provision of IFRs to clients can be contextualized within the broader issue of discretion, as a type of coping strategy. As decisions about possible paths of action are always embedded in a specific institutional and organizational setting, I portray here the broader context in which public services are provided. The literature points to three main factors that most prominently direct contemporary policy implementation at the street level: welfare reforms, New Public Management (NPM) reforms, and values of competing approaches such as New Public Governance.

2.1 Welfare Reforms and Diminishing Governmental Resources

Most Western societies have witnessed welfare reforms in the past few decades, influenced mainly by neoliberal ideology. These reforms have led to massive institutional changes in social policies and related policies, which are often perceived as dismantling the welfare state (Hacker, 2019). Notwithstanding cross-country variations, the reforms include freedom of markets and market-ization processes; championing values of personal responsibility and individu-alism; and restricted state action (Harvey, 2007; Maman & Rosenhek, 2011; Nieuwenhuis & Maldonado, 2018).

As states have been restructured to operate according to market rationalities, profoundly changing the nature of the welfare state, the social contract between the state and its citizens has also changed. Scholars explain that whereas earlier welfare regimes used access to various public resources and services as a main means of protecting citizens from possible harm from the free market, contem-porary regimes minimize the public safety net, reflecting withdrawal of the state's responsibility for its citizens (Hacker, 2019).

Most important in terms of policy implementation under these reforms is the component of massive budgetary cuts. Indeed, the problem of resources has always been integral to the implementation of public policy at the street level (Kosar & Schachter, 2011; Thomann, 2015). However, the difficulties and complexities in the contemporary work environment have been exacerbated by two consequences of the welfare reforms: (1) the adoption of austerity measures in the public services (Pollitt & Bouckaert, 2017), such that workers have fewer public/organizational resources to use in their daily work; and (2) escalating poverty rates and social inequality in many countries. Consequently, frontline workers who provide public services operate under conditions of increased demand and scarcer financial resources (Hupe & Krogt, 2013). Hupe and Buffat (2014) described these structural institutional constraints as a "public service gap" resulting from the large differences between the resources given to workers to fulfill their tasks and the actual resources needed to meet demand.

2.2 New Public Management

The second factor directing contemporary provision of public services is the work under NPM guidelines. Over the last few decades, NPM has been considered the dominant view in public administration (Pollitt & Bouckaert, 2017). This approach emphasizes economic rationality in the conduct of public administration workers. Core characteristics of NPM are greater reliance on market mechanisms; adoption and assimilation of private-sector approaches and management methods in the public sector; encouragement of privatization and outsourcing; and an emphasis on results and productivity (Moynihan, 2008). Key values in this approach are efficiency and effectiveness (see Pollitt, 2010 for further reading on NPM).

As the literature has demonstrated, the introduction of market-like mechanisms into the implementation of public policy has drastically altered daily work on the front line (Evans, 2016). As part of the decentralization approach, policy is set by high-level politicians and bureaucrats, while it is the responsibility of street-level organizations and workers to decide how to implement it (Brodkin, 2011) in a way that ensures economy effectiveness (Soss, Fording & Schram, 2011). Moreover, in the context of street-level work, NPM focuses on result-oriented rewards related to workers' performance, as well as treating recipients as "customers" rather than citizens (Bryson, Crosby & Bloomberg, 2014; Glinsner et al., 2019). New Public Management puts a strong emphasis on customer orientation while simultaneously introducing new forms of labor control: a system of performance measurement and benchmarking that has led to competition between administrative units and individual workers (Cohen, Benish & Shamriz-Ilouz, 2016). This transformation of public agencies fosters an "entrepreneurial spirit" (Bröckling, 2015), as workers are forced to compete for effectiveness and efficiency (Hartmann & Khademian, 2010; Moynihan, 2008).

To sum up, the public service gap created by welfare reforms converges with NPM economic values. Together with an emphasis on efficiency and client choice (Tummers, Steijn & Bekkers, 2012), the manpower and resources to achieve desired outcomes have been sharply reduced. Further complicating the situation for those who implement policy at the front line is an emerging new approach to public administration.

2.3 Public Value Governance

Alongside the dominance of NPM values, voices criticizing this approach have become prominent in the last two decades. These critics promote the assumption that government should not be run like a business, but rather as a democracy (Denhardt & Denhardt, 2015). The new approach, which does not have an agreed-upon label (Bryson et al., 2014), is represented in works such as Denhardt and Denhardt's (2015) New Public Service, Osborne's (2010) New Public Governance, and Boyte's (2005) call to reframe democracy. Such scholars, as well as others, maintain that the NPM focus on efficacy and effectiveness undermines other democratic values, such as inclusion, citizenship, and cultivation of the public sphere. This new approach highlights several main stances, including emphasis on public value and public values; a recognition that government has a special role as a guarantor of public values; belief in the importance of public management broadly conceived and of service to and for the public; and a heightened emphasis on citizenship and democratic and collaborative governance (Bryson et al., 2014). As part of this approach, policy implementation at the street level is expected to follow certain core principles: seeking public interest; valuing citizenship and public service above entrepreneurship; acknowledging the central role of frontline providers as serving citizens more than customers; and valuing people more than productivity (Bryson, Crosby & Bloomberg, 2015). In their symposium introduction on public value governance, Bryson and colleagues (2014) conclude that most of the main characteristics of NPM remain prominent and concurrent with the competing values of this new approach, creating a somewhat vague environment. It is not surprising, therefore, that this setting increases the ambiguity of daily work at the front line, compelling service providers to invent new ways of adequately doing their job (i.e., implementing designed policy).

2.4 Discretion and Coping Strategies

Today's frontline workers, regardless of the public service they provide (e.g., welfare, health, education), are confronted with the need to perform under the convergence of competing values of marketization, efficiency, and effectiveness, on the one hand, and public values based on citizens' needs, on the other. The constant demand to make decisions while implementing policy is considered an inherent characteristic of their work (Lipsky, 2010 [1980]). This is traditionally framed in the literature as "discretion," which has been defined as a fundamental feature of social service provision (Brodkin, 2006). In his classic book on street-level work, Lipsky (2010 [1980]) maintained that the uncertainties and constant work pressure with which street-level workers have to cope makes such discretion necessary.

One main aspect of these work pressures is related to the fact that street-level workers embody the point of interaction between the state and its citizens, as workers have a dual commitment to the state and their clients (Maynard-Moody & Musheno, 2000, 2003). The authors demonstrated that street-level workers use two types of narratives to describe their decision-making about policy implementation: as citizen agents and as state agents. While they did not present these narratives as dichotomous, in actuality, decisions made as citizen agents often contradict possible actions as state agents, and vice versa.

Ample literature has focused on the component of discretion at the front line, in an attempt to understand the coping strategies service providers use in their daily work. These efforts have increased over the last twenty years, as scholars and practitioners have come to realize that the environment in the public services is changing and that workers have to develop new ways of coping, implementing policy in a post-welfare reform era (just to name a few: Brodkin, 2011; Cohen, 2016; Dörrenbächer, 2017; Evans, 2016; Evans & Hupe, 2020; Gofen, 2013; Hupe & Krogt, 2013; Maynard-Moody & Portillo, 2010; Thomann, van Engen & Tummers, 2018; Tummers & Bekkers, 2014). The important insights yielded from these works reveal that although coping strategies are sometimes reflected in toughening practices and attitudes toward clients, frontline service providers often work hard to enhance the well-being of their clients (Evans, 2012), to "move toward clients" (Tummers et al., 2015), and to "do more with less" (Hupe & Buffat, 2014).

As more and more evidence has accumulated to support the tendency of workers to use their discretion in ways that emphasize their responsiveness to clients' needs, I have come to realize that two fundamental aspects of frontline service are not being addressed by the literature or fully understood. First, the literature maintains that discretion should be understood as a normative aspect of freedom and choice. However, as contemporary conditions *force* workers to employ discretion, is this not, in fact, a coerced element in their work? Second, if the contemporary institutional setting introduces such a constrained environment, how can workers *actually* deliver services to clients? In particular, how do they manage to provide resources in the absence of organizational ones? Resource scarcity does not allow workers to deliver designed policy; there are simply too few resources and too many needs. While "using discretion" seems to be the immediate solution, it can be overly simplistic when the math does not add up: too few and too many. Nonetheless, in interactions with clients, frontline providers *are* operating in *some* way. What do they do? What directs their decision-making and practices? These enigmas have led me to conclude that in order to understand the nature of public service delivery in the contemporary environment, I need new conceptualizations and I have to seek hidden practices enacted by workers that might provide some answers.

2.5 First Hints of Workers' Provision of Personal Resources

The majority of studies examining public service delivery at the front line have focused on workers' decision-making and discretionary practices with respect to the formal organizational resources at their disposal, as part of their formal policy work. However, a careful read of the literature suggests a somewhat latent aspect of service delivery, where workers provide services in ways that are above and beyond their formal role requirements. One major example is Dubois's (2016) work on welfare offices in France, which describes his six-month observation of face-to-face encounters between frontline reception agents and clients applying for family benefits. In his field notes, Dubois wrote, "Often, you get to play a role that goes far beyond what might be expected of a reception agent in a family benefit office" (2016:105). The practices which go beyond the formal role are embedded in the fact that the workers are physically engaged with clients (meet clients in person), which leads to personal involvement. These practices include giving technical assistance beyond the mere processing of the application, helping translate forms, spending more time than formally allotted to each client, and giving advice that falls outside the institutional framework based on personal experience. Dubois emphasizes the emotional support workers give to clients, as described by one of his interviewees: "You can listen to them if they have a problem with their son, or with their rent, even if there's nothing you can do" (2016:105). Support beyond the formal role is given against a backdrop of reduced formal resources, staff downsizing, and expectations to do "a lot more than we did five years ago" (2016:103).

Tummers and colleagues (2015), in their review of street-level workers' coping strategies, categorized the personal involvement that Dubois describes as "moving toward clients" by using "personal resources." Dubois's study was, in fact, the only one to fall in this category of coping. I became familiar with Dubois's work when I was struggling to understand the findings of my own study on social workers in welfare offices in Israel. Together with Roni Strier, I found that workers had to implement policy under "structural deficiencies" (Lavee & Strier, 2019) resembling the conditions portrayed in Dubois's French welfare offices and in the context of the "public service gap" described by Hupe and Buffat (2014), where street-level workers have to "do more with less," implementing policy against the backdrop of reduced organizational resources and growing citizens' needs. In our study of Israeli social workers who operate under conditions of increased client poverty and social policy that disregards clients' distress, social workers highlighted their interpersonal relationships with clients as their main tool in implementing policy. We found that workers used their emotions as resources provided to clients in place of traditional social benefits, as the latter were too limited to be of much assistance. We framed these practices as informal ones in which workers provide alternative personal resources to clients (Lavee & Strier, 2019).

Tummers and colleagues (2015) defined such personal resources as going beyond what is specified in the workers' job descriptions. Surprisingly, from the 277 texts they reviewed to map coping strategies, only 7 percent mentioned workers' usage of their own resources to assist clients. As I was trying to make sense of my own findings about the emotional resources that social workers provided to clients, and the personal involvement described by Dubois (2016), I was confused by the scarcity of such mentions in the literature on coping strategies. One possible explanation is that Tummers's review draws on studies published between 1981 and 2014. It is possible that, as the institutional context changes, workers' practices change accordingly. This insight can be inferred from Thomann, van Engen, and Tummers's (2018) claim that workers' discretionary practices are evolving under changing circumstances. Therefore, it can be argued that the environment described previously – in which a scarcity of formal resources coincides with concurrent values of NPM and new public governance – calls for a change in the traditional focus of discretion research on practices involving formal resources. When workers implement policy which itself is insufficient and does not provide an adequate response to citizens' needs, we need to delve deeper into the mystery of "what workers actually do" in their interactions with clients. It is my claim that a focus on the IFRs that workers provide to clients offers a comprehensive and nuanced explanation. To explore resources that are not formally provided by the organization, but are rather taken from the workers' own capital, I draw on Small's (2006:276) definition of a resource as "any symbolic or material good beneficial to an individual ... including economic or social capital, information, a credential, a material good, or a service, among other things." As such, informal resources are defined as any of the aforementioned resources that are provided by workers and are not part of their formal duties, or formal resources provided in informal ways.

3 General Design for Exploring the Hidden Tier of Frontline Service Delivery: Qualitative Method

The dearth of empirical attention to frontline workers' provision of personal resources to clients, in a context of highly limited formal organizational resources, might be attributed to difficulties exploring hidden discretionary decisions and practices with quantitative measures. Therefore, to explore these "beneath-the-surface" aspects of service delivery, I decided to employ the qualitative method of inquiry. The qualitative perspective entails delving deep into people's experiences, perceptions, and personal beliefs, as explained by Lincoln and Denzin (2003:3) in their classic work: "Qualitative research is a situated activity that locates the observer in the world.... [It] consists of a set of ... practices that make the world visible .... [Q]ualitative researchers study things in their natural settings, attempting to make sense of or interpret phenomenon in terms of the meanings people bring to them."

Embracing this approach, my basic premise is that, in order to explore the provision of personal resources as a phenomenon embedded in workers' experiences in their interactions with clients, I have to gain a comprehensive understanding of the meaning given to it by those who act within the explored reality. For this purpose, I have to study the phenomenon as a whole, across all its components. It is therefore crucial to examine the context of the phenomenon from a multidimensional and situational perspective. From this standpoint, linear relationships of cause and effect do not adequately explain the reality, and the main goal of the inquiry is to demonstrate the "social meaning" of individual perceptions and practices (Becker, 1996). Such nuanced exploration has ultimately allowed me to generate explanations that are sensitive to the context and most closely reflect the experiences of the human actors.

One of the basic weaknesses of qualitative research is its intuitiveness and subjectiveness compared to quantitative systematic methods (Denzin & Lincoln, 2008; Roulston, 2010). This impacts the generalizability and transferability of the particular case study to other cases. For the same reason, group comparisons are less common in qualitative inquiry, as it is challenging to reach decisive conclusions regarding similarities and differences. With this in mind, in planning and executing the studies presented here, I draw on several main criteria for quality in qualitative research (Tracy & Hinrichs, 2017), as well as my own experience conducting qualitative studies, in an effort to overcome some of the basic challenges in qualitative group comparison and to reach the highest scientific rigor. Several such elements have strengthened the quality of this study. First, the study design was constructed systematically, including all the steps of the research process. Second, the study draws on a wide sample, across three policy domains, several professional locations, various organizations, and three labor market sectors. Third, during the interaction with interviewees, the interviewers draw on the components suggested by Lavee and Itzchakov (2021) for good listening as a key element in enhancing the quality of the data and of the overall study. This richness of data allowed me to provide sufficient evidence to ensure credibility of the findings. Fourth, the size of the sample was not determined prior to the study, but was decided when I reached a point of saturation and no new data emerged (Small, 2009a). Finally, the analysis was conducted using computer software dedicated to analyzing qualitative data (Atlas.ti). The software allowed me to sort out the findings and find meaning without getting lost in the richness of the data. Most important in terms of comparative data, the software enabled a comparison of codes and categories across both policy domains and labor market sectors, as well as the ability to find interrelationships between categories, in a way that yielded solid theoretical arguments regarding similarities and differences between groups.

3.1 Studies 1 and 2: Methodological Procedure

3.1.1 Samples

To describe the nature of contemporary provision of public services, with a focus on the hidden tier of service provision, I drew on two samples. The first included 214 frontline workers from the welfare (N = 93), health (N = 56), and education (N = 65) domains in Israel, all employed in the public sector (Study 1; see Table 1). Interviews were conducted in 2016–19. All participants were street-level workers, according to Lipsky's (2010) definition: working as policy implementers in one of the three social policy domains mentioned and having direct daily interaction with clients. The majority were women (N = 170). Interviewees ranged in age from 25 to 60. In terms of ethnic distribution, 166 were Jews and 48 were Arabs.

The second study compared sectors. Interviews with 84 frontline workers from the public (N=35), nonprofit (N = 22), and private (N = 27) sectors were conducted in 2020–1 (see Table 2). Similar to the first study, the vast majority (63) of interviewees were women. As for occupations, 28 participants worked in the welfare domain, 26 in the health domain, and 30 in the education domain. Age and ethnic distribution were similar to the first study.

In both studies, participants were recruited from several organizations. With the help of research assistants, we used professional contacts in each

Table 1 Participants (N) by service domain and gender, Study 1

Policy domain	Female	Male	Total
Welfare	83	10	93
Health	34	22	56
Education	53	12	65
Total	**170**	**44**	**214**

Table 2 Participants (N) by sector, service domain, and gender, Study 2

Sector	Policy domain	Female	Male	Total
Public				
	Welfare	8	1	9
	Health	11	4	15
	Education	8	3	11
Nonprofit				
	Welfare	8	2	10
	Health	1	0	1
	Education	9	2	11
Private				
	Welfare	8	1	9
	Health	6	4	10
	Education	4	4	8
Total		**63**	**21**	**84**

occupational domain and approached key actors in each organization. We then asked them to refer us to potential interviewees who fit the inclusion criteria. Initial contact with most potential interviewees was by phone, where we introduced the study and requested their consent to participate. The research was described as addressing "relationships between frontline workers providing various social services and their clients."

3.1.2 Instrument

The instrument used was in-depth, semi-structured interviews. The interview protocol, which was similar in the two studies, aimed to comprehensively explore the daily experience of frontline workers, with a particular emphasis on the resources the workers provide to clients – both formal and informal. Participants were first asked to describe their normal work routine and the services they are required to provide to clients. They were then asked about the formal resources they provide to clients, in terms of organizational/governmental resources they have at their disposal, for the purpose of policy implementation. Finally, the main portion of the protocol was designed to comprehensively explore beneath-the-surface policy work. It focused on the informal services and resources (IFRs) that participants provide to their clients. These IFRs were explained to participants as *any resource they give to clients which go above and beyond the formal requirements of their job* – namely, that are not part of their formal duties, or formal resources provided in informal ways (after hours, off duty).

3.1.3 Procedure

The majority of the interviews in both studies were conducted face-to-face. Some interviews in Study 2 were conducted during the COVID-19 pandemic, when it was virtually impossible to meet, and so were held online, via Zoom software. All interviews were recorded and transcribed verbatim. Participants' anonymity and confidentiality were ensured, and all names and personal details were replaced by pseudonyms.

3.1.4 Saturation Points

The scope of the two studies, in terms of numbers of participants and the data yielded from the interviews, is relatively broad for qualitative research. My main reason for collecting so much evidence was to allow for the establishment of solid theoretical arguments. In designing and executing these studies, I adopt Michael Burawoy's stance on qualitative methods as my point of departure: according to Burawoy (1998), we can use qualitative methods (e.g., in-depth interviews) to extract the general from the unique, to move from the "micro" to the "macro." By investigating a social phenomenon within its context, followed by valid systematic analysis of the data that allows for the deduction of relations between several characteristics of the phenomenon, I could develop a theoretical explanation of individuals' reactions within a specific social context. Such an analysis allows me to extrapolate from one particular case to other contexts. In determining when I had "enough" evidence to allow for this extrapolation, I drew on Mario Small's (2009a) argument on saturation points (or, to put it in his words, "how many cases do we need?"). That is, I stopped when no unique cases emerged, when no exceptional cases were found that could contradict other findings, and when further cases did not contribute new insights to the theoretical argument.

In both studies, two saturation points directed the data gathering and analysis. In Study 1, the initial point of saturation was when the evidence demonstrated – in a way that could not be interpreted in any other direction – that frontline workers in all professional locations regularly provide a wide range of IFRs to clients. The broad database, which included various professions, organizations, and types of clients, allows me to argue that the provision of IFRs is a broad and solid social phenomenon. This initial saturation point was thus reached the moment I understood that further interviews would not contribute to or alter my theoretical argument about the existence of this phenomenon. However, as this was the first study to directly focus on under-the-surface practices on the front line, it was crucial to continue interviewing even after establishing the social phenomenon, in order to comprehensively understand the various manifestations of these informal practices and services. The final saturation point, after which no further interviews were conducted, was reached when new interviews did not provide substantially different examples of IFR provision, but rather reinforced what had been revealed in prior interviews.

In Study 2, the initial saturation point was reached when enough data was collected to demonstrate the scope of IFR provision in each sector and particularly the content of these IFRs. When the scope was clear and the content was repetitive in additional interviews, I stopped interviewing and focused on the analysis, on extracting the theoretical argument about emerging "particular role perceptions" (see my elaboration in Section 5). After establishing this theoretical argument, I continued interviewing frontline workers in the three sectors (about ten) to see if further data would expand upon or alter the theoretical argument. The final saturation point was reached when I completed the analysis of these additional interviews and realized that no further insights could be gleaned from the new evidence.

4 The Provision of Informal Resources in the Public Sector

The analysis of 214 interviews with frontline workers in the public sector revealed that the vast majority of workers do provide informal services and resources to their clients. Even though I anticipated this finding, based on insights from my previous studies, I was struck by the scope and intensity of the phenomenon as it emerged from the interviews. Not only did virtually *all* workers report providing IFRs, they also described such provision as a *routine practice*, as part of their daily policy work. For analytical clarity, I have divided the resources into three categories: (1) emotional resources, where workers provided psychological support to clients or maintained close relationships with them; (2) instrumental resources, where workers provided assistance with administrative or bureaucratic procedures, or gave advice or a consultation; and (3) material resources, where workers provided cash or cash-equivalent resources to clients.

It should be clarified that workers sometimes provided emotional, instrumental, and even material resources in their formal role. The difference is that informal resources were taken from the worker's own capital and not from organizational resources. Most often, IFRs were provided off duty and after work hours. In other cases, the offered IFRs were different than the formal resources workers had to provide, and went above and beyond their professional knowledge or skills.

Table 3 presents the types of IFRs provided by frontline workers, including a few brief examples. The table demonstrates the remarkable range of such resources in each type. Indeed, the different types of resources often overlap, and some subcategories could be associated with more than one type. For example, the IFR of "accompanying clients as they handle bureaucratic tasks," which is presented under instrumental resources, could also be categorized as emotional support, part of extra personal treatment. Similarly, the resource "giving rides in one's own car" could be categorized as either a material resource (money for gas) or an instrumental resource. Common to all types of IFRs is the large amount of time involved in the provision of these resources – both on and off duty. Table 3 provides several in-depth examples to illustrate the manifestations of each type of IFR.

Table 3 Informal resources provided by public-sector workers: Types and examples

Type of informal resource	Examples
Emotional resources	Emotional and psychological support (e.g., motivational talks)
	Inviting clients to the worker's home (for Friday night dinner and holidays)
	Extra personal treatment (e.g., giving out one's private phone number)
Instrumental resources	Assisting with bureaucracy (e.g., filling out forms, writing letters, translating forms)
	Accompanying clients on bureaucratic errands, during and after work hours
	Providing services to the client's family (e.g., help with job searches, assisting with appointments to professionals, providing medical exams for client's family members)
	Providing training and consulting unrelated to formal duties (e.g., teaching how to write a resume, guidance on educating a client's teenage children)
Material resources	Giving cash
	Buying things for clients and their families (e.g., food and other home necessities, medicine and other health-related materials, clothing and shoes, school materials)
	Giving rides in one's own car

(Table adapted from Lavee, 2021)

4.1 Emotional Informal Resources

The most common type of IFR provided to clients was emotional support and the maintenance of a close personal relationship. The main manifestation of emotional IFRs was the constant availability of workers. Workers from all professions (with the exception of nurses) reported giving clients their private phone number. This basically means working all hours of the day, every day, as clients take advantage of the opportunity to call the service provider any time. A social worker stated: "I give my private number to clients who I know are in distress, especially those I know are without support systems. They call me outside of work hours and of course I always pick up the phone." Another social worker said: "Everyone has my private number, and they all call and text."

For teachers, it is common practice to give their private numbers to both students and parents, as much of the formal work is carried out by phone, such as group messaging related to class materials, collective announcements, and the like. However, more than as a means of doing formal work, teachers linked their constant availability to emotional IFRs provided to clients. For example, a teacher said: "I spend hours on the phone, after work hours, on calls and with text messages, and calls again, hours upon hours, in order to encourage and push both my students and their parents."

Other aspects of emotional IFRs were provided during work hours, but were outside of formal role requirements. Although in some professions, emotional and psychological support are inherent to the formal job, the participants made a clear distinction between formal and informal emotional resources they provide to clients. For instance, a worker in the employment section of the welfare office said: "I do give clients a lot of psychological support, it's not professional or anything. But if I see they need it, I do it. Give them emotional support, listen to their problem. Then a meeting of an hour is spent empowering the client instead of employment training."

Similarly, a social worker explained:

> I'm not an expert in the area of psychology, but often I need to provide an emotional response, and I can't just shut the door on those who need it. Many times they really need someone to listen to them. I do it, and it's at the expense of my other obligations, and I have to spend time making up the so-called "lost" time.

Many workers explained that they provide IFRs in response to clients' needs for emotional support, as is clear from the words of a nurse:

> I often give an attentive ear or go the extra mile, beyond what I need [to do]. For example, there's a mother with a hospitalized child, and the father is

absent. She really needs the attention, so I check in with her two or three times during my shift to say "Hi, how are you doing?"

Another manifestation of emotional IFRs was inviting clients to the worker's home. A teacher stated: "I have a student I know whose mom is still at work most of the time he gets home from school. So sometimes he comes home with me and eats with my kids, plays with them, and later he goes home."

Another teacher expanded on this theme of giving students a sense of home:

> There are students who I invite to my home for Shabbat dinner, talk with them and give them a motherly feeling. There are students who talk to me for hours outside of school hours . . .. These are usually students from broken homes . . . with me they get a sense of home, a warm feeling.

Yet another teacher said there are students whose parents are unavailable. For them, she serves as both alarm clock and shuttle bus:

> It begins with calling the boy in the morning to wake him, and coming to his house to pick him up, and this goes on throughout the year, not just once or twice. I have two students who, if I hadn't picked them up from home in the last two years, they wouldn't have graduated.

The final example of emotional IFRs is unique. A physician said: "I have a patient who is obese, and I commit myself to participating with him in fitness training. He needs this motivation because otherwise he wouldn't go forward."

4.2 Instrumental Informal Resources

The second type of IFRs includes various kinds of instrumental assistance to clients. These entail, among other things, providing information, training and consultations beyond the requirements of formal duties. Workers also often assist clients with red tape: "I help some clients appeal to government agencies, such as the National Insurance Institute. I do all this outside my formal duties. I help them write letters, make phone calls and send faxes" (social worker).

Other social workers said:

> Several weeks ago, on my day off, I accompanied one of my clients to the bank. He has severe problems at home and can't understand the language properly, and he really needed my assistance to get all the forms he needs to receive financial support.
>
> I have a client whose electricity was cut off because she didn't pay the bill. She wanted to pay by check, and you can't do this over the phone except with a credit card. So, after my work day I went with her to the offices of the electric company, I know the manager there. He assisted us right away, she paid and could have her electricity back at the same moment.

Clients often perceive professionals as "experts" not only in their given fields, but also in the broader institutional system, and therefore approach them for advice and assistance in a wide range of areas. A rehabilitation worker said:

> I had a client, a mother, who was in severe financial distress. She didn't know what to do and asked for help. Although I should only assist her with employment-related issues, I called welfare, and they gave me a list of soup kitchens. So, she didn't know how to call them. I made a few phone calls myself, gave her all the information, told her exactly what to do.

The data analysis revealed that providing instrumental IFRs in the form of information that goes above and beyond the worker's particular area of expertise is highly common in interviews with doctors and nurses. Perceiving these workers as experts in the overall medical domain, clients frequently asked them for advice on various health-related issues – matters that went far beyond the specific service that the professional had to provide under formal role requirements:

> It happens all the time, patients seek advice or assistance in many things related to medical affairs, even if it's not at all related to the initial issue they came to get treatment for. For example, today I had a patient who asked me to connect him with a company that provides night nurses. It's not my job, but I'm still addressing all these things. (nurse)

Another nurse said:

> Some parents ask for guidance on all sorts of medical issues unrelated to me. I search for information, bring them brochures, check the articles online – all this I do at home, of course I don't have time to do this during my shift. A lot of times the information I find is in English, and then I also help with translation, because there are people who don't understand the language.

The words of a physician sum up the magnitude of this phenomenon: "There are thousands of people to whom I have given information above and beyond, assisting them in navigating the healthcare system, for my clients and also their relatives. These are things they were supposed to search for themselves, but couldn't find."

People who come for healthcare services are often in a vulnerable position, either ill or elderly, and find themselves in situations in which their condition could worsen if they do not receive further information. In these routine situations, workers' provision of instrumental IFRs is virtually inevitable:

> Yes, I find myself writing letters, or adding to the regular letter notes that can help my patients. I often find myself going down to the administrative office

> and explaining what forms and paperwork the patient should have, because the patient can't explain it himself. And I go through patients' documents that are not necessarily related to my field of medical expertise, and I try to explain what is important and what is not. (physician)

Similar to other professionals, healthcare professionals are perceived as part of the broader bureaucratic system, and as authorities who can assist with various bureaucratic matters:

> I help many clients fill out forms, not [just] medical forms, for instance, those who have been injured and want to apply for support from Social Security, to declare that the medical problem is the result of a work accident, and the like. Especially those who don't know the language or what rights they are entitled to. I help them. (nurse)

In the previous section, I demonstrated the broad informal emotional support that teachers provide to their clients – both students and parents. Even more so, many teachers reported providing instrumental IFRs. These were usually manifested as doing a formal job (i.e., teaching class material) in informal ways, mainly after work hours: "Often I tutor students who are struggling, on my own time and my days off."

The provision of this kind of instrumental IFR was reported as a routine practice more than as a one-time act: "Once a week I stay two hours of my own time after school hours to allow those who need it to come to me, individually or as a group, to get extra practice."

Other instrumental IFRs provided by teachers included searching for information about scholarships for students, explaining where to find information and how to apply, as well as seeing to the medical needs of students. For example, a teacher who noticed that her student did not see well made him an appointment with an optometrist. Another example entails brokering between students from low-income families and external organizations which could assist them, such as charity organizations that provide lunch vouchers or tickets to public transportation.

4.3 Material Informal Resources

Material resources that were provided to clients included cash and goods. The majority of teachers who work with economically weakened populations reported providing all kinds of material IFRs:

> I provide far beyond what I need to formally. At the beginning of the year, I buy notebooks, pens, and diaries for anyone who can't buy [them] on their own.

> I often find myself buying school supplies – pencils, notebooks, rulers. These are things that are basic for students.
>
> There are students who don't have school uniforms, food, clothes, bus money. I take care of them. I try to get all these from donations, but often it also comes out of my own money.
>
> Every year there are students I bring sandwiches to on a regular basis, because I know that even if I call their parents to say their kid arrived without food, it wouldn't help.

In the other professions studied, stories on providing material IFRs were less common and at a lower frequency (not on a regular basis) than in the education domain. Nonetheless, almost all social workers had examples:

> I was on a home visit and there was nothing in the fridge. I went to the supermarket and bought them groceries so they won't be hungry for the next few days.
>
> My job is not to give financial aid. But if I see that a child's condition is very bad and tragic, without anyone knowing it, I give him money out of my own pocket.

Summing up my findings about the provision of IFRs in the public sector, I would like to reemphasize that the typology illustrated here, in which I gave examples of distinct types of resources, is useful for presenting results, but is artificial in terms of street-level reality. In real life, as reflected in the interviewees' stories, workers do not provide just one type of IFR, but rather are engaged in varied informal practices, relying on their personal capital. The next excerpt – a teacher's response to our question about informal practices – offers a glimpse into the comprehensive nature of informal provision of resources:

> The first resource is time. I find myself looking after students after school hours and during recess, giving academic assistance or emotional support, all of which add up to many hours of work that I'm not compensated for. Another resource is school supplies that I buy for them if necessary and, in more difficult cases, [I] even buy clothes now and then for students who seem to have no one to provide it for them. I have close relationships with them and a strong sense of personal responsibility.

5 Provision of Informal Resources: Sector Comparison

5.1 Hybridity at the Frontline of Public Service Delivery

While public services have traditionally been delivered by public administration organizations, the macro-level changes described earlier – particularly welfare reform and managerial practices that draw on private-sector logic – have led policy implementation and public service delivery to be executed also by private and third-sector organizations (Benjamin, 2016). Even though the vast majority of organizations are divided by broad definitions into public, private, or nonprofit sectors, considerable research has demonstrated that the sharp distinctions made between these sectors mask the hybridity in many of the organizations (Fossestøl et al., 2015; Krøtel & Villadsen, 2016), such that public service delivery is characterized by organizational structures with mixed public, nonprofit, and for-profit characteristics (Smith, 2010). These include public–private partnerships, contracted-out service delivery structures, quasi-autonomous agencies, user-managed public facilities, collaborative forums of various types, social enterprises, and systems of network governance (Skelcher & Smith, 2015). Such hybridity causes organizations to resemble a skein-like coil that is difficult, if not impossible, to untangle.

While this complexity might be rooted in the contestation between competing logics (Skelcher & Ferlie, 2005), scholars tend to agree that the erosion of boundaries between public, private, and nonprofit organizations is strongly related to massive processes of marketization. This trend is manifested in competition for funding, which causes organizations across all sectors to adopt similar practices (Cohen et al., 2016). For example, both nonprofit and for-profit organizations receive public funds. Therefore, even nonprofit organizations are encouraged to compete for government contracts, through formal competitive bidding procedures. This introduces market competition even into the third sector (Smith, 2010).

A distinct stream of research within the hybridity literature focuses on workers' adaptation to the need to operate in complex hybrid environments (Pache & Santos, 2012), where policy implementation is infused with market principles across all sectors (Thomann, Hupe & Sager, 2018). Hupe and Hill (2007) argued that contrasting and even contradictory rules, norms, and social expectations may produce tensions in policy implementation, presenting ongoing dilemmas to frontline workers, particularly in their interactions with clients. Growing literature has demonstrated that frontline workers in all sectors have to balance the demands of the state and the market.

In addition to this general environment that influences workers' practices, beyond sectors, the literature also describes professional norms that are common to workers in the same occupations. Mainly, the sociology of professions, which defines a profession as an occupation with a certain kind of knowledge base (Freidson, 2001), highlights the importance of such professional norms. Defined as prescriptions commonly known and used by the members of an occupation (Andersen, 2009), these norms lead professionals in the same occupation to behave and perform similarly, regardless of their sector and incentives. Strong professional norms are said to influence workers' behavior and work performance, and can overshadow individual values and motivations (Bøgh Andersen & Serritzlew, 2012).

According to the perspective of the sociology of professions, these norms differentiate between workers according to their profession, even workers employed in different sectors. In this view, when it comes to workers' discretion about policy implementation, professional norms are likely to determine their practices more than any other trend. At the same time, however, professional norms may be subject to the structural changes made in the provision of public services. Indeed, contemporary public administration literature has demonstrated that these changes influenced and shaped workers' discretion and implementation practices in accordance with particular tensions and demands of the employment sector, beyond profession variations in similar sectors.

Structural changes in public service provision, and particularly hybridization, have also impacted workers' accountability. Traditionally, the accountability of public service providers was linked to three major sources of influence: formal state rules, professional standards, and societal expectations (Hupe & Buffat, 2014; Hupe & Krogt, 2013). However, in the contemporary hybrid environment, where public policy goals coexist with such market-led goals as efficiency and profit (Ebrahim, Battilana & Mair, 2014), the increased adoption of market mechanisms adds a fourth influence: market accountability (Thomann, Hupe & Sager, 2018). These multiple accountabilities can drastically intensify the tension in contemporary policy work, as frontline workers are "serving many masters" (Thomann, Hupe & Sager, 2018).

This multiplicity of demands, commitments, and values resembles the long-standing debate about state agent versus citizen agent narratives, beginning with Maynard-Moody and Musheno (2000). Based on the understanding that service providers in the three sectors vary in their sense of accountability, level of discretion, and the organizational resources available for providing adequate service, I argue that exploring IFR provision across these three sectors not only adds knowledge to contemporary debates on similarities and differences in service provision across sectors, but also provides a better sense of their commitments and a deeper understanding of which "masters" they serve.

5.2 Hybridity in Action: How to Differentiate between Sectors?

Today, basic public services – mainly in the welfare, health, and education domains – are provided not only by the public sector, but also by private and nonprofit sectors.[1] The first step in comparing sectors was thus to locate the organizations from which participants could be recruited.

---

[1]   The three sectors can vary in many characteristics, such as type of clients, available resources, and workload. This variation also occurs between countries and according to welfare regimes and social policies. In Israel, the three examined policy domains are relatively similar in terms of the type of client, but rather different in terms of working conditions. In the welfare domain, in all

Several days after I asked my research coordinator to locate potential organizations in Israel, she returned confused. Finding public-sector organizations was relatively easy, but when she tried to find nonprofit or private organizations it seemed like virtually no organization could be classified as purely nonprofit or private. We spent hours on the websites of organizations, trying to untangle their complex structures with the aim of determining the sector they belonged to. At first, we thought that tracing the money – discovering who funds the organization's daily operations – would provide a relatively simple answer. It soon became clear that, with the hybridization of social service provision resulting from the macro-level institutional changes described in previous sections (e.g., Moynihan, 2008; Pache & Santos, 2012; Pollitt & Bouckaert, 2017), funding for at least part of the operation of all these organizations was governmental. Moreover, all organizations that provide social services are subject to state regulations. Due to the requirement to meet certain criteria, the state not only funds the organizations and thus indirectly affects the financing of the organization's operations and workers' salaries, but often directly funds certain actions of the organization (i.e., a certain tier of the services is state funded), while other actions are funded by donations (in the case of nonprofits) or private money (in the private sector). A further complication is related to the fact that service providers in all three sectors have similar professional backgrounds. Teachers are teachers, nurses are nurses, doctors are doctors. Regardless of the sector, they are subject to similar professional rules, codes of ethics, and norms. As such, in all sectors, workers may be serving "many masters" and have multiple accountabilities.

Ultimately, we included in the study only those organizations whose definition, funding, and ways of operation allowed us to clearly associate them with a specific sector, excluding those whose hybridity was overly complex. We also made sure that the interviewees' understanding of the sector in which they were employed was consistent with the classification we made.

---

employment sectors, clients belong to weakened populations. In the education domain, the vast majority of schools belong to the public sector. However, within public schools, there are programs operated by private or nonprofit organizations. Consequently, there are no substantial differences between the clients (students and their parents) of teachers and other education workers in this study. Finally, in the health domain, all citizens are entitled to public health services, which are of relatively good quality. Thus, individuals from all socioeconomic levels obtain health services from the public sector. While there is also an expanding private sector, people from relatively lower socioeconomic levels can consume private health services at a fairly low price by extending their public health insurance. As a result, clients of public and private health organizations are not substantially different in Israel, unlike countries such as the United States where there is a considerable gap in the quality of public and private health services.

5.3 Analytical Procedure of Sector Comparison

When analyzing data for the public sector, I first coded all informal resources and services and then categorized them by type. As elaborated upon in Section 4, the categorization yielded three main types of IFRs: emotional, instrumental, and material. The data analysis allowed me to establish the existence of the phenomenon, to demonstrate its broad scope, and to present the vast range of IFRs provided by public-sector workers.

However, when exploring differences between public, nonprofit, and private sectors in terms of the types and scope of IFRs provided, the inductive analysis suggested that the division relevant to the public sector was not necessarily applicable to other sectors. At first, I thought I could examine the differences based on reports similar to those I had gleaned from the public sector. This would yield nine reports: three sectors times three resources. Results, however, indicated that while I could indeed find differences in the scope of resources provided in each sector (that is, the range of types of resources and frequency of informal practices), similar to the previous categorization, there were also differences in the content of resources. Moreover, crossing categories of scope and content revealed a key finding, which emerged only at this stage of analysis: the provision of IFRs is embedded in and shaped by different ration-ales, representing particular role perceptions of workers, that vary according to employment sector.

Therefore, the comparative findings presented in this section are divided into three meta-categories, in keeping with the three general types of resources found in the public-sector study: emotional aspects, instrumental aspects, and material aspects. These categories do not consist of particular types of resources (as in the previous study), but rather detail several subcategories in each meta-type. This allows me to go beyond the nuances of types of resources (over-resolution for the comparative study) toward a broader perspective, enabling a more accurate comparison between sectors in terms of scope and content. Ultimately, this kind of qualitative comparative analysis extracted a theoretical argument regarding similarities and differences between sectors. My main argument is that the differences in IFR provision are embedded in what I term *particular role perceptions*, which derive from values, norms, and expectations. These do not imply distinctions between individuals, who might have different personal beliefs and behaviors, or even nature-based tendencies to work in a certain sector, as has been suggested in comparative works (see for example, Baarspul & Wilderom, 2011; Christensen, Moon & Whitford, 2021), but rather point to differences shaped by the values, norms, and behavioral expectations in each employment sector. In what follows, I present the gist of the most essential characteristics of the particular role perception in each sector and demonstrate how these perceptions are manifested in each sector and each aspect of IFR provision.

5.4 Particular Role Perceptions

5.4.1 Public Sector: Public Representative

The provision of IFRs in the public sector is embedded in the values, norms, and expectations of an amalgamation of state agent and citizen agent, as termed by Maynard-Moody and Musheno (2000, 2003). Under the role perception of public representative, public-sector workers understand themselves as responsible for citizens' well-being. This derives from their role as public servants and as part of the general mission of policy implementation. Here IFRs are provided through the individual worker's personal responsibility to fill the gap created by insufficient governmental or organizational resources. As part of this perception, the individual worker does not represent a specific profession or organization, but rather the "system" as a whole – the larger institutional network. In keeping with this perception, the resources provided go above and beyond the formal and relatively narrow definition of their particular role. This perception requires, by definition, constant hard work, as workers take it upon themselves to compensate for the withdrawal of state responsibility, investing enormous efforts to ensure citizens' well-being.

The provision of IFRs in the public sector is not part of the worker's formal role requirements, and the resources themselves are part of the worker's personal capital. Under such role perceptions, there is a clear distinction between formal and informal resources, and provision of the latter is coerced in the absence of formal resources.

5.4.2 Nonprofit sector: Humanity Representative

The role perception of workers in the nonprofit sector is embedded in the premise that, despite their professional location, which places them in a higher power position than their clients, the interaction with clients is between two human beings. In other words, they aim to generate a nonhierarchical relationship. Thus, the worker is a humanity representative (taken from humanistic terminology), perceiving each citizen/client as a whole person rather than seeing them through the narrow lens of their particular needs. As such, the implementation work in a specific domain draws on the understanding that the provision of services must acknowledge clients in a comprehensive and holistic manner.

In the nonprofit sector, IFRs are intentionally provided separately from formal resources. The former are presented as part of human commitment between people, regardless of the availability of formal resources. Thus, IFRs are offered as a tool, with the aim of fostering this point of view among clients as well, encouraging less-formal relationships. Moreover, workers provide resources which deliberately diverge from formal role requirements so as to highlight the contrast between flexible and creative nonprofit organizations and the archaic, limited, and narrow public sector.

5.4.3 Private Sector: Organization Representative

The role perception of workers in the private sector is as representatives of the specific organization in which they are employed. This is not the same as market accountability. When describing the provision of IFRs, workers usually avoid terms that could imply reliance on market-related values such as increasing competitiveness or effectiveness. Rather, the informal practices are enacted for the benefit of the organization and as part of providing good service – not only by the individual worker, but as part of the general interest of the organization.

While there is a clear distinction between formal and informal resources, the premise is that despite practices being informal (not part of the formal role definition), they are still part of the job. Therefore, IFRs are provided not due to a scarcity of organizational resources, but in order to demonstrate the worker's extra commitment to clients and to position the organization as providing better services than other organizations.

5.5 Variations in the Provision of Informal Personal Resources

This section presents the main findings of the sector comparison analysis, divided into three meta-categories and their related subcategories. The meta-category of emotional aspects can generally be described as containing all sorts of emotional resources and services that are informally provided by workers to clients. These are not tangible or concrete resources, but rather involve various practices aimed at enhancing clients' emotional and mental well-being.

The meta-category of instrumental aspects contains various manifestations of informal practices enacted to assist clients and enhance their ability to reach a certain goal or desirable purpose. The instrumental resources and services are therefore tangible in the sense that they are targeted for use by clients. They are not as amorphous as the emotional aspects of IFR provision, but they are less concrete than the material aspects.

Finally, the meta-category of material aspects includes various ways of providing clients with goods of monetary value, either cash itself or cash equivalent. These practices are meant to enhance clients' ability to cope with economic hardships. They involve provision of the workers' own material resources as well as workers' brokering practices for recruiting material resources from others.

In the remainder of this section, I provide examples of similarities and differences between employment sectors in terms of the scope and content of IFRs for each meta-category. A summary of the comparative analysis is presented in Table 4.

5.6 Meta-category: Emotional Aspects

5.6.1 Extra Personal Treatment, Informal Support, and Availability

All subcategories under the meta-category of emotional aspects are presented together. This is different from the other two meta-categories, under which I present each subcategory separately. I combine the emotional aspects because the rationale for the provision of resources and services for all these subcategories were very similar, such that differentiation between them proved unnecessary.

- Sector comparison: Broad provision of IFRs related to emotional aspects by workers from all sectors.
- Similarity in scope; difference in content.

5.6.2 Emotional Aspects, Public Sector

Rationales for providing emotionally related IFRs in the public sector were mainly embedded in constrained situations, resulting from the gap between *inadequate formal resources* and *commitment to provide adequate services to clients*. As such, the informal practices were described as coerced. Such coercion is reflected in the words of a teacher:

> Many students approach me during breaks, and if I don't have enough time, I ask them to come at the end of the day and stay with them after work hours. You know that in a class of 40 students you won't be able to allocate the necessary individual time for everyone, so I have to give them solutions at the expense of my personal time as well. This is not only about explaining the material, but also about educating them well, such as enhancing their self-esteem.

A social worker expanded on the constrained organizational environment, characterized by lack of time and a massive workload: "There is tremendous time pressure, a feeling I never have enough time for my clients. So I have to

Table 4 Summary of IFR sector comparison: Scope, content and rationale

Meta-category	Subcategory	Similarities/ differences between sectors	Sector comparison: Scope of provision	Sector comparison: Rationale of provision
Emotional aspects	Extra personal treatment Informal support Availability	Similarities in scope Differences in content	**Public sector:** Broad provision **Nonprofit sector:** Broad provision **Private sector:** Broad provision	**Public sector:** Organizational constraints: substituting for inadequate formal resources Commitment to citizens/clients Role constraints (such as lack of time) force provision No formal response **Nonprofit sector:** Outside-the-box practices; deliberate deviation from formal job definition Holistic perception of clients Means of establishing personal relationships, bridging the gap in the formal power hierarchy Highlighting the contrast to the formal public system **Private sector:** The informal is part of the formal Providing extra good organizational service Promoting organizational interests: positioning the organization as better than others

Table 4 (cont.)

Meta-category	Subcategory	Similarities/differences between sectors	Sector comparison: Scope of provision	Sector comparison: Rationale of provision
Instrumental aspects	Facilitating procedures Assisting with bureaucracy	Differences in scope Differences in content	**Public sector:** Broad provision **Nonprofit sector:** Little provision **Private sector:** Minimal provision	**Public sector:** Response to clients' perception of the bureaucratic system as a single unit **Nonprofit sector:** Supplementing formal services Highlighting difference from formal public sector
	Other services not part of formal work	Similarities in scope Differences in content	**Public sector:** Broad provision **Nonprofit sector:** Broad provision **Private sector:** Broad provision	**Public sector:** Organizational constraints: insufficient formal resources Everything relates to everything: commitment to assist citizens as public representatives Increasing clients' trust in the system **Nonprofit sector:** Holistic perception of clients, addressing various aspects of clients' lives Commitment of one human being to another Commitment of the powerful to the powerless Deliberate differentiation from the narrowmindedness of public services

Material aspects	Recruiting material resources from others	Differences in scope	**Public sector:** Broad provision **Nonprofit sector:** Little provision **Private sector:** Minimal provision
		Differences in content	**Private sector:** Perceiving the role holistically; informal practices as part of the role Market rationality of competition: providing unique and distinct services Demonstrating organizational commitment to clients **Public sector:** Compensation for insufficient funding of public institutions Coerced provision resulting from gap between organizational resources and clients' needs **Nonprofit sector:** Supporting informal activities
	Providing personal material resources	Differences in scope	**Public sector:** Little provision **Nonprofit sector:** Minimal provision **Private sector:** Minimal provision
		Differences in content	**Public sector:** Compensation for insufficient formal resources Commitment to clients' well-being **Nonprofit sector:** Random cases, assistance of one person to another **Private sector:** Assistance given informally by organization and not from worker's own capital

give of myself even after work hours, at times when I'm supposed to be with my children. There isn't enough time and you must respond to people's needs."

These excerpts begin to uncover how the informal practices of public-sector workers are embedded in their role perception as public representatives. The interviewees acknowledge that formal organizational resources do not allow them to provide the necessary response to clients' needs. Understanding themselves as responsible for their clients' well-being, they supplement inadequate formal resources with their own personal resources.

Many social service providers deal not only with the clients they come in direct and daily contact with, but also their family members, who are essentially indirect clients. As the formal workday usually does not include service provision to these indirect clients, the interaction with them is often carried out as informal practices, which are essential in order to supplement the formal work. For example, teachers describe how the school system does not recognize the massive and frequent relationships they have with parents. As formal implementation work is done in the classroom or in the general school area, these workers must provide personal resources which are manifested in various emotional aspects, such as availability after work hours or emotionally supporting the parents:

> Most of the day I'm in class with the students, so I have to do all the other things after work hours, like making phone calls to parents, reassuring parents, parents often need you to reassure them about their child. Often they simply need emotional support for problems with their children that are not directly related to my class or even to school.

Another main rationale for providing IFRs, found across all professional locations in the public sector, was a strong feeling of *commitment to clients*. Teachers related that they regularly devote many hours in the afternoon and evening to phone calls with students and their parents, explaining: "I feel committed to them" and "I can't not take their call, I'm committed to them and each time I tell myself this could be a critical call." Similarly, a doctor said: "I have some patients with complications to whom I'm very committed. I give them my personal mobile number and my personal email, at which I'm always available."

The sense of commitment of public-sector workers stands in sharp contrast to the lack of formal resources. Workers explained that the organizational response is not sufficient to implement policy in a way that ensures their clients' well-being. Thus, it is in fact a sense of commitment that forces workers to provide personal resources, as is demonstrated in the words of a hospital nurse:

> We always have time pressures. They want the OR to be occupied all day long, so there are no breaks between surgeries. Often I stay after work hours

because the system is not built to really respond to patients' needs. For instance, if there's a patient who I know is a more complicated [case], then as an experienced nurse I'm also very committed to my patients, so I'll stay with them on my own initiative. I know they need support that goes beyond what the hospital formally provides.

Another aspect, related to the public-sector workers' sense of commitment and the coercion to provide IFRs, is the understanding that there is *no formal response to the emotional needs* of clients in current public services (beyond those whose formal objective is to provide emotionally or psychologically related services). As public representatives, these workers embody an amalgam of both state agent and citizen agent. Representing a broader institutional system whose overall role is to ensure citizens' well-being, workers explained that they must fill the gaps with their own emotional resources, as a nurse maintained: "I give a lot of extra personal care to many of my patients, who need this extra emotional support. I do it because I know that if not for me, no one will give them this support."

The necessity to provide emotional resources is intensified by the inadequacy of formal mental health services, as expressed by a social worker:

> For example, there's a girl in whom I see all the signs that she's getting depressed and there's a risk of suicide, so I have to keep her together, I have to answer her calls or visit her at home. The mental health system won't give her an adequate response because she's considered only low risk, but I can't ignore her.

5.6.3 Emotional Aspects, Nonprofit Sector

Nonprofit workers often explained the provision of emotionally related IFRs as *intentional deviation from the formal job definition* by engaging in *practices that are "outside the box."* The following excerpt is from an interview of a social worker in a nonprofit organization whose formal role is to provide welfare services to low-income families. This woman created a youth soccer team, through which she wished to provide clients with emotional tools:

> I sometimes try to get a little out of the box we are used to because I think we have other tools in the box that we can use. And the best example of a case in which I have deviated from the formal definition of my role is that I started a soccer team for some of my clients' kids. I do it outside of routine work and regular work hours, and I see it as a tremendous achievement. I see it as therapy through soccer that goes beyond what is formally known and as emotional support for teens.

As humanity representatives, a central value of nonprofit workers that leads them to provide emotional IFRs is to *perceive clients in a holistic way.* An employment consultant told of a client who was anxious about taking public transportation, but could not afford his own car. The worker explained that she understood how integration of her client in the labor market required addressing his anxiety problem, even though this is an emotional issue far beyond her formal role, which focuses on employment. Therefore, she and a colleague "just rode with him on the bus a few times, and then very carefully one of us got off at another stop in order to allow him to stay on his own for one stop. When we saw it was okay, we let him ride two stops alone and so on, until he could get over the anxiety. It was important to me that he return to normal functioning."

The various emotional resources provided by workers in the nonprofit sector were also related to their willingness *to bridge the gap in the formal power hierarchy*, in which, as professionals, they are located in a higher position. A teacher said:

> Actually, I'm available all the time, even during hours and days when I'm not formally working. I do this so my students know they can contact me any time, that it's not just a teacher–student relationship and that there is never a time that I just cut them off and am unavailable.

Lastly, the analysis revealed that a central rationale of nonprofit-sector workers to provide informal emotional resources is to *highlight the difference between nonprofit and public sectors*, as expressed in the story of a social worker at a nonprofit organization that provides services to people with disabilities. The worker related that she accompanies clients to job interviews in order to give them emotional support in such a stressful situation. By doing so, she is deliberately violating formal government instructions:

> I admit that I do it despite Ministry of Health guidelines, and I even intend to write to the Ministry of Health, because it is their instruction that clients should not be accompanied to job interviews. Personally, I think it would be unprofessional on my part to do that, because it hurts my clients. I feel uncomfortable, somewhat cold, to tell her that my job goes only so far, and from here on you are on your own.

5.6.4 Emotional Aspects, Private Sector

Although the difference between formal and informal practices is well acknowledged, the main explanations that private-sector workers gave for providing emotionally related IFRs were rooted in the norm that *the informal is part of the formal*. This is salient in the words of a teacher:

> [I give] mostly time, a great deal of investment of time beyond formal school hours. The teacher's involvement is part of the educational conception here,

and it's not something unusual, it's the way things work. If, for example, in the summer there are children who need some more preparation for next year, I meet them and go over the material with them. It's during my vacation and of course without any extra pay.

Similarly, a nurse working in a private clinic explained that unpaid practices are still part of the job: "I often have very long talks with patients or family members in the evening, and as I said earlier, I don't get paid for it, but I can say that I see it as part of my job."

A social worker in a private facility for adults with autism disorder described how she was always available to the residents' parents:

It's hard to know where the work starts and where it ends, which means it's really a twenty-four seven job even though I officially finish at five. That is, if parents really need me – often they worry and need to be reassured that everything is OK – they know I am [on duty] twenty-four hours. They know I'm available all the time, which means that even when I'm not here, I'm here.

Later in the interview, the same social worker linked being available all the time to the central value of *providing extra good service* to clients:

In all humility, in my opinion and not only in my opinion, we are really better than others. I work the way I do because I'm always available to parents even at unreasonable hours. No one can complain that I don't answer at 10 pm. They can always get a response.

Contrary to values and motivations which are considered internally induced, such as public service motivation for public-sector workers (Perry & Wise, 1990) or intrinsic motivation for nonprofit-sector workers (Leete, 2000), private-sector workers highlighted the centrality of good service as a general organizational norm that shapes their understanding of the need to provide IFRs. This is expressed, for example, by a nurse who avoided relating the extra personal treatment she provides to clients' families to an internal personal perception of good service. Using the term "right" service instead of "good" service may imply an organizational expectation to provide IFRs: "When a new case comes in, I accompany the families from start to finish, and although I don't have to, I give them, for example, tours around the place to calm them. It's very important for the caregiver to give the right service to families."

Following these norms of behavior, the next two excerpts demonstrate the understanding that *informal practices position the organization as better than others* and therefore are performed *to promote the organization's interest*:

I don't feel like I work by the hour, but [rather] work by emotion, by my dedication to clients. If, for instance, a patient is being released after my work hours, I stay, build a plan for him, check the situation with his family, and I think that this relationship leverages the organization. (nurse)

My patients have my phone number and they can reach me in any situation and at any time. This is certainly not the case with all doctors, but with us it is, to the best of my knowledge, we strive to be very available to our patients. This is something we bring here, and you should remember that this is not the case everywhere. (physician)

5.6.5 Emotional Aspects: Summary

To sum up the meta-category of emotionally related IFRs, the analysis demonstrated that the provision of a vast array of personal resources related to emotional aspects is common across all three employment sectors. However, the rationales for the informal practices varied considerably between workers from different sectors. While the main rationale among public-sector workers was presented as coercion linked to inadequate organizational resources, and the motivating values were commitment to citizens, these aspects were mentioned much less by workers in the other two sectors. In the nonprofit sector, IFR provision was primarily shaped by values of the commitment of one human being to another, and in the private sector, it was shaped by values of commitment to the organization.

5.7 Meta-category: Instrumental Aspects

Two subcategories were revealed with respect to the instrumental aspects of IFR provision. The first focuses on facilitating procedures and assisting with bureaucracy. The second refers to other aspects of informal work unrelated to bureaucratic procedures.

5.7.1 Facilitating Procedures and Assisting with Bureaucracy

- Sector comparison: Differences in both the scope and the content of IFRs.
- Public sector: road provision; nonprofit sector: little provision; private sector: minimal provision.

5.7.2 Facilitating Procedures and Assisting with Bureaucracy, Public Sector

Interviews of public-sector workers demonstrated that they provide a large amount of assistance with bureaucratic issues. Such assistance is informal in that it either is within the workers' area of expertise yet not part of their formal role, or in areas unrelated to their job or profession. The analysis revealed that these informal practices were done first and foremost *in response to clients' perception of the bureaucratic system as a single unit.* As such, clients expect "bureaucrats" to be able and willing to assist in all kinds of bureaucratic matters. For example, a nurse said:

> There are people who come to the clinic and think that they will get all the answers to their medical problems here. They ask you to do all sorts of things, and you see people who are lost and in distress and so you help them. For example, there was a couple here who couldn't understand the language. I translated the Hebrew documents into Russian, and after that they didn't know where to go and where to make an appointment, so I started calling all sorts of places to understand where they should go and wrote everything down for them, who they need to contact. In the end I also made the call for them.

Many nurses and doctors reported that clients often ask for advice on general medical matters, unrelated to the particular issue addressed or service they are receiving from the professional worker. Clients often asked for recommendations of doctors, clinics or services in other areas of expertise, advice on treatment they received in other places, and medical recommendations for family members.

In many cases, it seems that clients not only perceive the "bureaucratic system" as a single unit, but also assume that professionals in one area are experts in other professions as well – perceiving them as a single body with the authority to assist in varied domains. Thus, nurses found themselves filling out applications for social rights, teachers facilitated bureaucratic procedures (e.g., in committees of the National Insurance Institute that determine eligibility for social support and various government allocations), social workers assisted clients with legal matters, and so on. This is reflected in the words of a teacher:

> I have a student with behavioral problems, and his parents asked me to be involved in the therapeutic process, even though it's not my responsibility. Because I intervened, I was able to facilitate intensive meetings with the welfare services, and I was able to quickly improve his physical and mental condition.

Similarly, in response to clients' requests, many other interviewees said they use personal connections to facilitate procedures – within or outside their area of expertise. Other interviewees related that clients assume workers in a specific organization have knowledge about or are able to influence all matters in the organization. For example, clients of welfare departments in local municipalities often ask their case workers to talk with workers in other departments of the municipality and to facilitate various procedures there.

The practices reported here demonstrate the amalgam that shapes public-sector workers' role perception as public representatives. Responding to clients' needs in various matters within the bureaucratic system, workers adopt not only the citizen agent narrative, but also the state agent narrative. Representing the larger institutional system, they feel responsible for taking care of citizens' needs. The informal services and resources they provide are indeed beyond their specific role, but are still within the broader mission of ensuring citizens' well-being.

5.7.3 Facilitating Procedures and Assisting with Bureaucracy, Nonprofit Sector

The instrumental aspect of IFR provision with respect to procedures and bureaucracy was mentioned only a few times by workers in the nonprofit sector. Of these, the informal services were mainly directed at facilitating procedures, while almost no mention was made of assisting with bureaucracy. This lack of assistance with bureaucratic matters stands in sharp contrast to the massive needs of citizens for such help, as was demonstrated by the stories of the public-sector workers. It is possible that workers in the nonprofit sector refuse to provide such services as part of their deliberate attempt to differentiate themselves from the public sector.

The provision of IFRs in the form of facilitating procedures was rationalized as essential for *supplementing formal services*. A nurse explained:

> I do all kind of things to speed up long procedures. For example, today I filled out a Nursing Law form for a client who lives in an assisted living facility. Then it turned out there's a section that needs to be filled out by the manager of the housing facility. I didn't want this person to have to wait, so I called the manager and got permission to sign on his behalf.

Similar logic is demonstrated in the words of a social worker who works in a nonprofit charitable organization. She told of how she uses her connections with the public welfare department to facilitate procedures:

> Sometimes people come for an intake meeting. But in order to open a file for them, they need to bring an approval form from their case worker, and sometimes they don't know they need to get the approval. So instead of waiting for them to make an appointment with her – this could take weeks – and only then send me the forms, I call her straight away, she faxes me the approval, and I can approve their entitlement to our services at the same meeting.

By providing such IFRs, the social worker ensures a prompt response to clients' needs. The quick solution to the bureaucratic burden allows the worker to *highlight the difference* between the complex, archaic public sector and the flexible, creative nonprofit sector.

5.7.4 Facilitating Procedures and Assisting with Bureaucracy, Private Sector

Almost no manifestations of this subcategory of instrumental aspects of IFR provision were found among private-sector workers. This might be due to the basic nature of private-sector organizations, in which procedures are naturally prompt and bureaucracy is minimal, particularly compared to the public sector. For example, if clients need to wait months for a doctor's appointment in public health services, the availability of appointments in the private sector is much greater, such that there is no need to facilitate procedures.

5.7.5 Other Services Not Part of Formal Work

• Sector comparison: Similarity in scope of IFRs, broad provision across all sectors; difference in content.

I present this aspect of the meta-category of instrumental IFRs separately from the previous subcategory, even though facilitating procedures and assisting with bureaucracy are also services provided beyond formal work. However, whereas the previous subcategory was mainly demonstrated by public-sector workers, the current one was broadly found among workers of all sectors. Moreover, the rationale for the provision of "other services" is different.

5.7.6 Other Services Not Part of Formal Work, Public Sector

Similar to the rationales for the provision of emotional aspects of IFRs, the most prevalent rationalization among public-sector workers for providing instrumental services that are not part of their formal role was related to *lack of sufficient formal solutions*. As such, workers are forced to provide informal services. This is expressed by a nurse working in a public clinic:

> We have patients coming for an examination, and then they need further treatment elsewhere and need to make an appointment or get assistance at another clinic. I have to respond even though it's not my job. I do it because there's no one else on the clinic staff whose job it is to do it. There are no administrative services, for example, even though they are required on a daily basis.

Similarly, another nurse reported that she feels forced to provide informal emotional support in the absence of formal services: "I actually function sometimes as a psychotherapist, mostly to do with patients' anxieties. If there was a social worker or psychotherapist here, it wouldn't fall on me; these pep talks are beyond my time and my knowledge." This excerpt also exemplifies how emotional resources are often instrumental and, in any case, go beyond the worker's professional training or formal role.

In feeling responsible for expanding the formal services and therefore compelled to provide informal services, public-sector workers demonstrate their commitment to citizens. However, as public representatives, rationales for providing services that are not part of the formal role were also expressed as the worker's desire to increase client trust in the "system" as a whole. A teacher justified the long hours she invests in students, beyond work hours and at the expense of her private time: "First and foremost, I do it in order to make students want to come to school, rather than lose their trust in the system."

A large number of public-sector social workers reported assisting clients with various issues unrelated to their work. Many mentioned that they help clients search for jobs or deal with employers. They explained that they do so in order to increase their clients' trust in authorities and their willingness to ask for and accept assistance that is necessary for their well-being. This is mainly true for particularly weakened populations, such as single mothers in poverty:

> Many people, and especially poor single mothers, are still having a hard time coming to the welfare department. For them I do a lot of things beyond my formal job, so that trust can be established – for example, when someone needs counseling on issues related to their children's learning disabilities or help to find the correct educational facilities. I don't want to tell her that I can't help her, because then I'll lose her.

The social worker is not worried about her personal relationship with the client, but rather afraid of her client's disconnection from the larger institutional system. This position is highly interwoven in the public representative role perception, in which the individual worker does not represent a specific profession or specific organization, but rather the "system" as a whole. As public representatives, *they are committed to assist citizens* even on matters that are only remotely related to their formal role.

Many teachers reported that, beyond their educational role, they also function as the "local welfare department" and engage in various practices to enhance the well-being of their students and the students' families. Common practices were purchasing home necessities and arranging food donations. The next excerpt is typical of interviews with teachers:

> There is a fourth grader who I teach English to, his parents are divorcing, and they are in great financial distress. For them I am also a social worker, because

his mother constantly has to work and has no time for other things. I looked for donations for them, for example of clothes and furniture. I spoke to the people at the municipality so they would link them up with charitable organizations.

This story demonstrates how various kinds of IFRs are intertwined. The instrumental services cited in the quote go beyond the formal services required from the workers, and can also be classified as material informal support.

5.7.7 Other Services Not Part of Formal Work, Nonprofit Sector

Embedded in the overall role perception of nonprofit-sector workers as humanity representatives, the general rationale for providing services that are not part of the formal role highlighted the *holistic perception of clients, addressing various aspects in clients' lives* which are unrelated to the worker's formal role or service. Thus, a social worker in a nonprofit organization explained her provision of instrumental IFRs as "obvious":

Beyond working as a social worker, I'm also an English teacher, and sometimes clients ask for my help with English. For example, many search for information on all kinds of topics on the Internet and find it only on English sites, so obviously I help those who need this assistance.

Another social worker, who is employed in a nonprofit organization that deals with food insecurity, maintained:

The women for whom I provide services need support in many issues, and I don't want to tell them, for example, "I'm only responsible for this and that." So, I will help a woman with a lot of issues beyond the food insecurity stuff. To name just a few cases – enrolling the children in school, helping them find treatment for children with learning difficulties, looking for jobs, and more.

While public-sector workers explained their provision of "other services" as embedded in their commitment as public representatives to citizens, nonprofit-sector workers perceived interactions with clients as much less hierarchical and as the *commitment of one human being to another*. As such, the boundaries between "formal" and "informal" services are blurred. This position is exemplified in the words of a public-sector nurse:

At some point you become part of the family, and then you can't say that something is not yours. There are many families for whom I go beyond my formal role and do other things. Let's say a family is suddenly in a crisis unrelated to my job, so should I refer them elsewhere? It just feels wrong.

At the same time, even when workers wish to maintain nonhierarchical relationships with clients, the nature of their positions as providers of necessary services to many coming from weakened populations creates inevitable power relations between worker and client. In keeping with this understanding, nonprofit-sector workers explain their wish to leverage this position to assist clients in various matters as part of a *commitment of those holding relatively powerful official positions to those who are less powerful*. This rationale is reflected in the words of two teachers:

> [I provide] assistance in finding the correct neurologist and assistance in searching for a job for the head of a family of one of my students. I'm committed to them by the very fact that I'm in some position of power and can help them with a variety of issues.
>
> For me this is a commitment. In my belief, I see the students beyond what happens in the classroom, I see them as a whole person. And as an educator, I'm committed to producing a broad supportive framework for them.

One central element which emerged repeatedly and profoundly in the rationales of nonprofit-sector workers for providing such informal services was *deliberate differentiation from the public sector*. A social worker who used to work as a senior manager in the public sector lengthily explained her desire to deliberately diverge from her formal role and provide clients with informal services as a way of distancing herself from her previous position:

> Before I came here, I worked in the Ministry of Welfare in a senior position, but I felt like a clerk, writing reports all day. Even though I was a civil servant with tenure, with everything, I felt that I couldn't stand it anymore, I couldn't work with these stupid systems. You bang your head against the wall and you have no ability to make your own statement . . .. In the civil service you can't change anything, you're like a horse in blinders and you only see forward, focused on going straight ahead. Here I'm not just focusing on the so-called formal matters, I have come to change what I can. That's why I'm here.

5.7.8 Other Services Not Part of Formal Work, Private Sector

Whereas workers in the nonprofit sector perceive clients in a holistic way, the narratives of private-sector workers suggest that they perceive the role holistically, such that *aspects not included in the formal role are still considered part of the job*:

> I had a patient who suffered terribly at 10:00 at night. She called me to say she had nowhere to buy medicine. Clearly, on the level of the formal job definition, I just need to give her the prescription. But in my opinion, we also need to bring her to the point where she's taking the medication, so I brought it to her at 10:30 at night.

This physician's words indicate a clear distinction between formal and informal practices. Like other workers in the private sector, and as part of the role perception as an organizational representative, the interviewee says "we need," using the collective pronoun instead of the singular "I." This understanding of the self as representing the organization often emerged from private-sector workers' descriptions of blurred boundaries between formal and informal resources.

This stance was also strongly related to the value of *providing a unique and distinct service to clients*, as a nurse who works in a private clinic described:

> If a mother is hospitalized with a baby after giving birth, she is completely alone because the father might be working or with the other children. She really needs the attention, so you go in two or three times a shift and ask her how she's doing. You help in some way. It may not be part of the job, but I can say to her, "Mom, go get some air, have a cup of coffee, come back in 20 minutes, you can leave the baby with me." It's a service they don't provide elsewhere, and it completely changes their experience.

Workers in the private sector not only maintained that the informal element allows them to emphasize the unique service of their organization, but also linked the IFRs to their *commitment to provide better service to their clients*. This norm of behavior is manifested in the words of a social worker: "I sometimes join activities that I'm not obliged to join, and I do it because of my commitment to the clients, so they know I'm always here for them. I bend the boundaries and try very hard to be available, even outside of regular work hours."

Similar to workers in the nonprofit sector who emphasized the difference between themselves and public-sector workers, workers in the private sector also explained that informal practices are done to distance their organization from outdated public-sector organizations. The IFRs allow them to portray the organization they work for as *providing innovative personal treatment, in contrast to the (inadequate) service they would receive from the public sector.* Two physicians in private facilities explained:

> Unlike public hospitals, here we sometimes work more to support and provide explanations to the families than to treat patients.
>
> Pediatricians in public clinics treat children separately from other family members, and see only them. But here, in my opinion, they get a relatively unique service because there are a lot of young families, and we have so-called informal conversations with the rest of the family, and this is our advantage. We see the overall scope of the problem and see also the ramifications for the entire family, more than seeing just the child or just the parents.

5.7.9 Instrumental Aspects: Summary

To sum up the meta-category of instrumental aspects, the analysis first demonstrated that there is considerable differentiation in types of instrumental resources provided by workers from each sector. While the provision of all kinds of instrumental resources was common among public-sector workers, based on their role perception as public representatives who are responsible for citizens' well-being, workers in the other two sectors demonstrated totally different patterns of IFR provision. First, very few nonprofit and private-sector workers reported assisting with bureaucratic procedures, with some even deliberately distancing themselves from being involved in such matters. I interpret this trend as reflecting the desire of nonprofit and private-sector workers to emphasize their distinction from the public sector. In contrast, workers from all three sectors were highly engaged in providing all other kinds of instrumental resources and services above and beyond their formal role. Their rationale for such broad provision, though, was different in each sector: public-sector workers emphasized their commitment to clients as citizens; nonprofit-sector workers provided instrumental IFRs as part of the humanistic commitment to clients as people; and private-sector workers provided extra-role services as part of their commitment to the organization and a desire to portray their organization as providing extra good service.

5.8 Meta-category: Material Aspects

The analysis yielded two material aspects of IFR provision: recruiting such resources from others and providing personal material resources. On the whole, the provision of resources falling under this meta-category was reported much less than the vast provision of IFRs reported for the meta-categories of emotional and instrumental aspects. Yet, even within this reduced provision, variations were found between sectors.

5.8.1 Recruiting Material Resources from Others

- Sector comparison: Differences in both scope and content of IFRs.
- Public sector: broad provision; nonprofit sector: little provision; private sector: minimal provision.

5.8.2 Recruiting Material Resources from Others, Public Sector

Various informal practices involving the recruitment of resources from others were reported across all professional domains within the public sector. The main rationale for these practices was the necessity to *compensate for the insufficient funding of public institutions*. The following excerpt is typical of what many teachers reported:

> I had two families whose financial situation was difficult and who couldn't buy a computer for their children. So, I asked the school principal to help them, but he said he can't because he has a very limited number of free computers. I tried to convince him, but in the end I turned to an organization that donates computers and got [the children] computers.

Similarly, a social worker explained that she has to make up for resources that used to be provided by the organization, but are no longer formally available due to budget cuts. As clients' needs have not been reduced, the workers have to search for these resources – in practices that go beyond their formal role:

> Every year before Passover, I go to a lot of department stores and ask them to donate holiday gifts to needy families. It's not part of my job at all, but if the welfare department once used to give shopping vouchers before the holiday, today they no longer give them out. So, I have to search for donations.

Such practices were most salient in teachers' and social workers' stories. Many of them devoted a large amount of their personal time to brokering practices, such as arranging events to get donations from parents, the community, and even their own social network. A teacher said: "I ask parents on a regular basis to donate clothes, books and school supplies for needy students." A social worker reported: "Often I recruit resources in informal ways. For example, many families need a computer for their kids. This is something for which I'm always looking for donations."

These practices were enacted as *coerced, created by the gap between organizational resources and clients' needs*. A social worker said: "A young woman gave birth and didn't have a changing table. This is not something I can get her from the welfare [department], so I arranged for a friend of mine to give her a suitable dresser." One social worker laughed at our probing into the brokering practices she described at length, saying that her friends tell her they can become social workers themselves, as they constantly engage in welfare-related activities, such as searching for donations, donating things themselves, assisting in moving furniture donated to families who have no car to pick it up, and so on.

Strangely enough, although public-sector workers devoted a great deal of their personal time to compensate for the absence of formal resources, the vast majority did not turn needy clients down by saying they just did not have the required resources, nor did they express resentment of the inadequate organizational response. Acting as public representatives, public-sector workers constantly work hard to shoulder the withdrawal of state responsibility. Constituting part of the "system" while taking responsibility for citizens in need, they just "do what needs to be done" to ensure citizens' well-being.

5.8.3 Recruiting Material Resources from Others, Nonprofit Sector

The material aspect of IFR provision was rarely mentioned by nonprofit-sector workers. The main rationale for recruiting material resources from others was *to support other kinds of informal activities*. For example, a teacher said: "I recently wanted to take my students to an escape room, so I recruited a donor to fund the activity." Similarly, the social worker who started a youth soccer team to provide clients with emotional tools (see the meta-category of emotional aspects of IFRs, Section 5.6.3) reported how she worked to find financial resources to support the team's activities: "I always try to reach all kinds of possible sponsors." The rationale these nonprofit-sector workers present for recruiting material resources from others points to practices that are mainly voluntary. This is much different than the coerced nature of the provision of this kind of IFRs by workers in the public sector.

5.8.4 Recruiting Material Resources from Others, Private Sector

The analysis of interviewees in the private sector found virtually no mention of recruiting material resources from others. There are several possible explanations for this. First, clients of private-sector organizations, even those organizations that provide social services, may be better off financially than clients of the public or nonprofit sector and therefore have fewer emergency needs than others. Second, whereas public-sector workers perceive themselves primarily as responsible for citizens' well-being, private-sector workers do not. While the extra-role services they provide, as described in the previous sections, indeed assist clients, these are primarily aimed at enhancing the organization's image rather than helping people in need per se. Many such services were initially provided to distinguish the organization from the public sector. As "we are not the welfare department" was repeated in various forms across interviews with private-sector workers, it is possible these workers intentionally do not seek to provide IFRs of a material nature.

5.8.5 Providing Personal Material Resources

- These IFRs were the least provided by workers in all sectors.
- Sector comparison: Slight differences in scope, differences in content of IFRs.
- Public sector: little provision; nonprofit sector: very little provision; private sector: minimal provision.

5.8.6 Providing Personal Material Resources, Public Sector

As opposed to all other kinds of IFRs, for which little differences in scope were found between professional domains in the public sector, it was teachers who mainly reported the provision of personal material resources. Many told of purchasing various kinds of school supplies for students, such as schoolbags, notebooks, and books. Also common was the provision of clothes, mainly school uniforms or shoes, as well as giving children lunch money. For example:

> According to school policy, there's one day a week when all the children buy lunch in the school cafeteria. One day at lunchtime, all the children left except for one child who stayed in the classroom. I know he comes from a family with a difficult financial situation. Without a second thought, I gave him money to buy food.
>
> There's a case of a poor family, where the father passed away, and the child lives with his mother and two younger brothers. Often I pay for him for all kinds of school events, such as trips or other activities, and I don't tell him, because I know his family can't afford these payments.

In other professional locations, social workers also reported providing their own material resources to clients. However, this was mainly for a particular one-time situation, such as giving someone money for public transportation or buying a warm coat for the winter.

As demonstrated by these examples, the main rationale for public-sector workers (i.e., teachers) to provide material IFRs on a regular basis is *workers' commitment to their clients' well-being in the absence of adequate organizational formal resources*. Teachers found school policy particularly irritating: the very same system that requires parents to pay for various extracurricular activities does not provide adequate solutions for those who are unable to afford these payments. The system ignores the fact that there are families who cannot meet these economic demands, and it ignores the common practice of teachers providing financial assistance to students.

5.8.7 Providing Personal Material Resources, Nonprofit Sector

The analysis revealed very little provision of personal material resources by nonprofit-sector workers to their clients. Such help was *random* and described as *assistance of one person to another*. Similar to the public sector, it was mostly teachers who reported offering such resources. One said: "If a student needs pencils, for example, I can provide them, or if someone is very hungry, I can give them a snack of an energy bar."

The dearth of personal material resources provided to clients stands in stark contrast to the clients' needs, as described, and to the vast range of other informal practices enacted by nonprofit-sector workers. Drawing on the practices described in the previous sections, and in line with the "out-of-the-box" thinking that characterizes the role perception of nonprofit-sector workers, it is possible that they struggle to find other solutions to material needs. In their deliberate distancing from the public sector, they do not perceive themselves as directly responsible for their clients' financial situation. Perceiving clients holistically, they may prefer to invest time and energy in providing comprehensive emotional and instrumental informal assistance, rather than helping with a more local or limited matter.

5.8.8 Providing Personal Material Resources, Private Sector

Private-sector workers, who rarely mentioned recruiting material resources from others, also made minimal mention of providing their own material resources. When workers in such organizations did report provision of material IFRs, they used plural pronouns, referring to "we" more than "I." For example, a teacher said: "I have a student whose family is really poor, so we bought him new school uniforms [and] candy, for him and also for his brothers."

In other cases, informal material assistance was given *from organizational resources rather than the worker's own capital.* For instance, a social worker described "a student with ADHD who forgot his wallet at home and couldn't pay for the ride home. I took money out of petty cash so he could go home."

The next excerpt, taken from an interview of a social worker, exemplifies that the relative availability of organizational material resources makes the worker's material IFR provision redundant: "My manager knows that if I ask for money for something related to clients, I do it because it has a professional agenda, it meets someone's need. So I have the organization's credit card and I can use it when I need to."

5.8.9 Material Aspects: Summary

The quote of the aforementioend social worker is ideal for concluding the meta-category of material aspects. The private-sector worker's account stands in stark contrast to the work conditions that characterize the public sector. As the resources of public-sector organizations become scarcer, front-line public-sector workers who interact with clients assume overall responsibility for them. In the absence of formal resources, they substitute their own resources.

The descriptions in the previous section also demonstrate the hierarchical relationships between workers and managers in the public sector: even when workers approach managers with requests for material support for clients in need, the reply is often negative. Assuming that the need remains until a solution is found, the responsibility for finding a solution remains at the level of the individual worker. In contrast, the relatively flat structure and low level of hierarchy in private-sector organizations allow workers to exercise their discretion in ways that not only provide clients with immediate assistance in emergency situations, but also do not place the burden on the shoulders of individual workers.

5.9 Conclusions Regarding Comparison

The sector comparison has shown that frontline workers across all three employment sectors – public, nonprofit and private – provide IFRs. However, the sectors are differentiated from one another in IFR provision much more than they are similar, in terms of both the scope of provision and the content of resources. Utilizing a theoretical categorization that draws on the grounded theory method of analysis, I was able to delve deeply into the sector comparison and set the basis for my key theoretical argument: namely, the rationale for IFR provision is embedded in the values, norms, and expectations of each sector, which, in turn, shape workers' role perceptions. Differences in the content and scope of IFRs provided are thus guided by different role perceptions.

Summing up, the analysis demonstrated that even if the vast majority of frontline workers provide IFRs, there are substantial differences between sectors. The bottom line is that public-sector workers provide a broader range of resources than those in the nonprofit or private sectors. Moreover, they are engaged in informal practices more as a coerced response to organizational constraints than from free will.

6 Implications of Informal Resources: Costs for Workers

Thus far, I have demonstrated the broad provision of IFRs by frontline workers to clients, as well as the varied aspects and types of resources they provide. I have also linked the scope and content of IFRs provided by workers in each employment sector to the particular role perception that distinguishes that sector. I now aim to uncover some of the possible consequences of IFR provision. Specifically, I focus on one main ramification, among many possible others: the costs for workers associated with the provision of their personal resources.

Ample literature has examined the consequences associated with demands and work-related burden embedded in the frontline worker's formal role (e.g., Destler, 2016; Giauque et al., 2012; Hsieh, 2014; Lavee & Strier, 2018; Steijn & van der Voet, 2019). These studies found various negative costs in terms of workers' physical and emotional health, such as burnout, fatigue, and increased stress. Much less is known, however, about the costs associated with practices that are not part of the workers' formal role, such as the informal practices examined here.

In light of the lack of knowledge about the costs of IFR provision, and in order to understand those costs within the framework of literature on the costs of extra-role practices, one possible option is to frame IFRs as an aspect of organizational citizenship behaviors (OCBs). These are discretionary behaviors that are not part of the formal requirements or reward system of the organization, but that promote organizational effectiveness (Organ, 1988). Although OCBs are usually considered positive behaviors, motivated by prosociality (Bolino & Grant, 2016) and benefiting the organization and its workers (Lyons & Scott, 2012; Whiting, Podsakoff & Pierce, 2008), a recent substantial line of research has also revealed the significant costs associated with these behaviors (Bolino et al., 2013; Bolino & Turnley, 2005). Thus, drawing on knowledge from the field of OCB may shed light on the costs associated with IFR provision.

Although OCBs are usually directed at other workers or the organization itself, they can also be directed at customers, which is known as citizenship behaviors oriented at customers (OCBCs). These behaviors, to name a few, can include being exceptionally courteous to customers, providing service quickly and with extreme care, speaking up for customers, and getting involved in issues that affect customers (Lam & Mayer, 2014; Ma & Qu, 2011). In line with the general definition of OCBs, these are practices that go beyond what the job requires formally.

6.1 Known Costs of Extra-Role Practices

What are the costs of practices that go above and beyond formal role requirements? Regardless of the target of behavior (coworkers, the organization, clients), studies have found a variety of costs related to extra-role behaviors (Bolino et al., 2013). There are OCBs costs for workers in terms of increased workload, general job stress, and even work–family conflict (Bolino & Turnley, 2005). Moreover, engaging in OCBs has been shown to interfere with perceptions of work goal progress (Koopman, Lanaj & Scott, 2015). The costs in time and energy associated with engaging in these behaviors often outweigh the benefits in the sense that those resources invested in helping others are at the expense of the workers' sanctioned task performance and can potentially endanger their career success (Bergeron, 2007). We find OCBs can also reduce workers' job satisfaction, especially when performed at very high levels and by individuals low in optimism (Munyon et al., 2009). Such OCBs can even have negative effects on group-level job performance, particularly when the task does not entail much interdependency between coworkers (Nielsen, Hrivnak & Shaw, 2009).

Drawing on this knowledge about costs associated with behaviors that go above and beyond formal role requirements, I, together with my colleague Shani Pindek, an occupational health researcher, analyzed the data of the 214 interviews of public-sector workers (Study 1) to explore the costs related to the provision of IFRs (Lavee & Pindek, 2020). We found that the wide range of IFRs provided by workers to clients (described in Section 4) resulted in a broad range of costs to workers. Our analysis revealed various aspects of emotional, physical, and material costs, as summarized in Table 5.

The most prevalent costs associated with IFRs were the impact on the workers' family lives, namely, their relations with partners and children. This was mostly due to the extra time devoted to clients and their continuous availability to them. Personal costs – which directly affect workers themselves (beyond reduced time and energy for children and partners) – were next in terms of frequency. First and foremost, the analysis indicated the informal resource of time investment in clients to be the highest cost for workers. Aspects of such costs are a loss of free time outside work, blurred boundaries between work and home, and absence of personal time during work hours.

Other prominent personal costs were physical exhaustion and emotional burden, which were often described together. Most interestingly, while the literature commonly describes physical and emotional exhaustion among service providers, particularly among those who provide social services, the participants in our analysis emphasized exhaustion in relation to informal practices more than to formal job requirements. Other personal costs were reported as economic costs, which were linked to the provision of material

Table 5 Costs associated with the provision of IFRs,
public sector*

Type of cost	Manifestations of costs
Familial costs	Availability to children
	Relationships with partners
Personal costs	Reduced free time
	Physical fatigue
	Emotional burden
	Material/economic costs
Professional	Time taken from other clients
	Reduced in-role performance

* Adapted from Lavee & Pindek, 2020.

IFRs. However, very few acknowledged that they paid a material price for providing material resources to clients. The last type of costs associated with the provision of IFRs was professional costs: the investment of IFRs in clients often impeded workers' ability to adequately meet their formal work requirements. This type of cost, however, was least mentioned by interviewees.

6.2 Workers' Perceptions of Costs: A Cross-Sector Analysis

In Section 5, which compared the provision of informal resources across employment sectors, I demonstrated that IFR provision in the public sector is first and foremost a response to organizational constraints and is often framed as coercion more than a choice. Framing informal resource provision as a type of organizational citizenship behavior, coercion to provide such IFRs can be understood as compulsory OCB (Vigoda-Gadot, 2006, 2007). Vigoda-Gadot argued that some extra-role behaviors are not based on the genuine goodwill of workers, but rather emerge in response to external pressures in the workplace. While he emphasized the influence of significant and powerful others, such as managers and coworkers, in coercing individuals into extra-role behaviors, such external pressures can be of various kinds. In such cases, OCBs are nonvoluntary practices. From the standpoint of the provision of IFRs, such pressures can result from the scarcity of formal organizational resources.

The theory of compulsory OCB argues that such practices may result in higher job stress, intentions to leave the organization, and burnout, as well as to lesser job satisfaction and weaker formal performance (Vigoda-Gadot, 2007). They can also lead to reduced creativity (novel and useful ideas) among workers (He et al., 2020), greater exhaustion (Nordhall et al., 2020), and turnover intentions (Yildiz & Elibol, 2021), to name but a few possible outcomes.

In the context of comparing costs associated with IFR provision, these are likely to vary between sectors. Such differences might be embedded in the finding that, in contrast to the compulsive, nonvoluntary nature of IFR provision in the public sector, such coercion was found to a much lesser extent (if at all) among workers in the other two sectors. I therefore assume that differences along the continuum of coercion–choice in providing IFRs will result in different understandings about costs associated with these informal practices.

To examine this assumption, I conducted a different analysis than the one done in Study 1. In both, I explored participant's replies to the question: "Are there any costs – in terms of personal costs or other costs – associated with the provision of the [earlier] described informal resources?" However, whereas in

Study 1, the analysis aimed at mapping the various types of costs that public-sector workers described, in the comparative analysis of sectors (Study 2), in accordance with the emerging different role perceptions, the analysis examined *workers' perceptions of costs*. My aim was to unpack the ways in which workers in the three sectors understand the costs associated with their informal practices.

The analysis revealed that, in line with differences in role perceptions, considerable differences were also found in workers' reports on costs. Particularly, their perceptions of the meaning of these costs varied in accordance with the sector in which they were employed.

6.2.1 Costs for Public-Sector Workers

The analysis revealed that public-sector workers believe their informal practices exact a very high price. Questions about costs were raised relatively late in the interview, after asking about provision of formal resources and then an extended probe of IFR provision. When we finally got around to costs, interviewees seemed unable to wait to reply, their eagerness expressed in extended answers and multiple examples. Apparently, this particular section of the interview raised strong feelings among these workers. Public-sector workers discussed these costs directly and explicitly, and their statements were punctuated with such phrases as "very certain" and "definitely." Here are some examples of the direct link they made between the provision of IFRs and the high costs:

> There's no doubt it makes me more irritated.
> The costs are extremely high.
> I invest a lot of my time, and the costs are comparable.
> It's just a waste of my time, or in other words, my private time that I can just rest.
> These resources take a lot of energy and time, and exhaust me a lot.
> It consumes a lot of time and valuable personal resources.

One of the main emphases interviewees placed on costs was their perceived duration: they indicated that the costs of providing IFRs were not local or momentary, but more persistent and constant. This was first and foremost linked to the frequency of the provision of IFRs, which in turn exacted frequent costs: "Often I'm not available to my family."

Beyond their frequency, the analysis revealed how comprehensive the costs were, impacting many of the people in workers' lives: "There are many negative consequences for me and my children"; "I pay a high price all the time. It drags your kids into the work, your entire family." The words of a teacher clearly express how deeply the family is affected by the large amount of extra time and energy invented in clients:

> Sometimes my husband laughs and tells me it might have been better to send our children to learn in my class, because in class I would give them more attention than in our home. It's a joke, of course, but I invest many hours in students at the expense of my afternoons, evenings, Saturdays, and holidays – time I'm supposed to be spending with the children and the family.

The informal practices drastically expand the formal role, in ways that cause workers to be involved with work far beyond what is required in formal role definitions. Such role expansion, and the considerable time invested in clients above and beyond formal work hours, create a fusion of private life and work life that is difficult to untangle. In the words of one interviewee: "You're at work all the time. At night you dream about students; work and life are mixed together; there's no such boundary as 'no, I'm not at work.'" Another said: "It constantly permeates my private life. Clients are always in my thoughts."

In sum, public-sector workers' replies indicate that the broad provision of IFRs by the vast majority of such workers is associated with ongoing costs. The workers are well aware of the price they pay for investing their personal resources, describing such costs as high and endless. Similar to their understanding of the provision of IFRs, these workers seem to perceive the price they exact as coerced; the element of choice was rarely mentioned in their stories.

6.2.2 Costs for Nonprofit-Sector Workers

Interestingly, the language that workers in the nonprofit sector used to describe the costs associated with IFR provision was completely different than the language used by public-sector workers. The most salient distinction was between the absolute and explicit manner in which the latter perceived costs and the much more implicit manner in which costs were described by nonprofit-sector workers. Rather than referring to "constant costs" and "high prices," those in the nonprofit sector often used such terms as "sometimes" and "little," for example: "Yes, there are some costs" or "Sometimes I feel like I'm paying a price for the extra time." Similar to public-sector workers, they reported personal and familial costs, but with a less extreme impact: "Sometimes I arrive home late, to the dissatisfaction of my family members, who really understand the need to invest the extra time in my clients."

Moreover, the descriptions of costs, when they arose, were often coupled with descriptions of satisfaction. Such linkage of satisfaction to costs may cause the price to be perceived as less heavy, mitigated by a sense of fulfilment. A social worker explained:

> It can be annoying at times. Sometimes you're at the cinema and there's a phone call from a client, and you say to yourself maybe it's not appropriate, and then you decide whether to pick up or not. In the end, I say okay and I answer. Still, you have this good feeling that you solved a problem, that you didn't leave anyone up in the air with any [unanswered] question or anxiety.

Another major difference was that nonprofit-sector workers perceived having a choice about paying the costs associated with IFR provision, as opposed to the coercion perceived by public-sector workers. For example, a teacher in the nonprofit sector said:

> I give more than I should in exceptional cases, and sometimes there is an accumulation of exceptional cases. At times like these, I decide upon the best way to act: do I really want to invest beyond what is required of me? And sometimes, if I feel that all the "beyond" stuff harms the quality of my [formal] functioning, I decide not to go beyond.

Finally, of particular interest in the context of choice versus coercion, a main theme emerging from the analysis of nonprofit-sector workers' stories is their belief that they can cease provision of IFRs whenever they decide to, when the price becomes too high for them to pay:

> If I notice that it happens at the expense of my children, I set a limit. For example, there was one phone call at midnight between Friday night and Saturday, and my kid got very scared. I felt really bad about it and I drew the line. First priority is to protect my own home. Since then, I have set a limit not to answer phone calls at night. If it's an emergency, they can call the emergency center.

6.2.3 Costs for Private-Sector Workers

The perceptions of private-sector workers about the costs associated with IFR provision differed both from those in the public sector and from those in the nonprofit sector. Their references to these costs were tinged with ambivalence, weaving direct, explicit descriptions (like those of public-sector workers) with more hesitant, implicit descriptions (like those of nonprofit-sector workers).

Similar to workers in the public sector, those in the private sector openly acknowledged the costs associated with their provision of IFRs. But in contrast to the endless costs described by public-sector workers, they used such terms as "maybe" and "sometimes," more like nonprofit-sector workers. In addition, private-sector workers did not perceive the costs as high, but more commonly as bothersome: "This is definitely inconvenient sometimes."

This quote demonstrates well the ambivalent manner in which workers in the private sector replied to questions targeted at understanding their perceptions of the costs associated with IFRs. The worker boldly stated there are "definitely" costs, but immediately qualified this by adding "sometimes." Moreover, these costs for providing IFRs – whether definite or just sometimes – are said to be "inconvenient," which carries much less weight than references to "high prices."

Another typical example of the ambivalent perceptions of private-sector workers about costs is found in the next quote: "Maybe time. Time is a huge resource. Sometimes it sucks you in very deeply." Similar to the previous one, this citation combines various perceptions of magnitude and frequency. The sentence begins with the reservation of time "maybe" being a cost, then moves to the understanding that the extra time invested in clients is a "huge" resource, yet the frequency is described as far less intense – "sometimes."

In addition, similar to the nonprofit sector, descriptions of costs tended to minimize them and emphasize the benefits: "There is a danger and a price you pay, but I do it wholeheartedly [literally, with fun]." Another interviewee, a private-sector social worker, likened the provision of IFRs to a chocolate addiction, the good feeling of eating sweets and the bad outcome of having too many:

> Yes, I pay a personal price, myself, my children, my family. That's on the one hand. On the other hand, I say, it's a bit like chocolate. You know it's unhealthy for you, but the feeling's a bit addictive, but also sucks a bit. On the one hand, you get pissed off. On the other hand, I succeeded, helped, assisted, even though it's really beyond my work hours. It gives [me] a different sense of satisfaction.

Private-sector workers often highlighted their satisfaction to justify their willingness to accept the costs exacted by IFR provision: "It brings me to less pleasant and comfortable places, but it feels good, also gives me satisfaction," said one. "These are costs in terms of time and emotional exhaustion. I feel good about investing more, even though it's exhausting; at the end of the day I feel immense satisfaction," said another. By closely linking costs and satisfaction, the price of providing IFRs was perceived as relatively low. In the words of another private-sector worker: "It's clear that sometimes I miss all sorts of personal things at home or in my personal studies, because I'm busy with work matters even during my private time. It's something negative, but I don't think it causes me any great harm."

Finally, like workers in the nonprofit sector, private-sector workers believed they have control over the costs of IFR provision; they can decide whether they are willing to pay the price or avoid it. The issue of choice was often highlighted:

> Certainly, there are prices, both personal and familial. When I have time, I do much more and beyond, but I can decide that at a certain time I'm not available for it, and the investment beyond is reduced.
>
> The main resource I provide informally is my time and it's costly, but it's also my decision: what yes, what no, when yes, when no, where I want to give and where not to give.

6.2.4 The Price of Coerced Costs versus Choice

An overview of social service providers' perceptions of the costs associated with providing IFRs to clients reveals a main difference between workers in the public sector and those in the nonprofit and private sectors – namely, the aspect of perceived choice and control over the price they pay for investing their personal resources. Interviewees in the nonprofit and private sectors maintained that when they feel costs are too high for them personally or for their families, they set a limit upon the informal practices that incur these costs. In contrast, public-sector workers rarely alluded to the element of choice. This perceived lack of control may explain the high frequency of costs in the public sector, described as "constant," and may be strongly related to their inability to set limits when the price is too high.

Stepping from the conceptualization of extra-role behaviors as compulsory (Vigoda-Gadot, 2006), the difference in workers' perceptions of costs exposes a dark and destructive side of IFR provision. The question that immediately arises is: What happens when public-sector workers want to draw the line, to put a limit to these high prices? If the provision of IFRs is not voluntary, but rather coerced, this means that one cannot choose whether to provide personal resources and, accordingly, cannot control the costs. For these workers, the only choice may be between keeping their job in the public sector or leaving for other sectors, where they might have more control over their own resources. This dilemma has far-reaching implications in terms of service provision in the public sector, which is discussed in the following section.

7 Conclusions: Challenges in the Contemporary Provision of Social Services

Contemporary provision of public services is made under the converging conditions of welfare-state reforms, NPM reforms, and values of competing approaches such as New Public Governance (Bryson et al., 2014).

These conditions shape the contours of contemporary work at the front line, determining how policy is implemented and how discretionary decisions are made. The main aim of this Element has been to explain "what workers actually do" in their interactions with clients, given conditions that create a widening gap between citizens' needs and policy response (Hupe & Buffat, 2014). I suggested that a focus on the IFRs that workers provide to clients might offer a comprehensive and nuanced answer to this question. The findings of the two studies reported here underscore the crucial role of personal resources provided by frontline workers, as part of their strategies for coping with changing institutional circumstances.

Drawing on two large-scale qualitative studies of frontline Israeli workers who provide welfare, education, and health services, the findings exposed the often unrecognized component of informal service provision across all sectors and professions of public service provision. Such evidence of the prevalence of the overall phenomenon of IFR provision is a major contribution to the literature, which has relatively ignored informal under-the-surface practices. A further significant contribution, enabled by highlighting this informal component, is deciphering how workers in different sectors adapt to the need to serve "many masters" (Thomann, Hupe & Sager, 2018) and revealing how multiple, sometimes contradictory, imperatives and values shape workers' specific role perceptions, which in turn shape service provision.

The mere phenomenon of IFR provision may have far-reaching consequences for workers, clients/citizens, public administration, and society in general. One aspect is the costs imposed on workers, which were empirically demonstrated in Section 6. I now discuss several additional implications of IFR provision involving the consequences for clients/citizens, ramifications for the broader public administration, and the gender meaning of informal practices. The section concludes with some suggestions for future policy.

7.1 How Does the Provision of IFRs Influence Clients/Citizens?

Are clients/citizens better off receiving workers' personal resources as opposed to not receiving them? In the two studies reported here, I only interviewed workers and so lack direct evidence from clients. However, I can make certain deductions about the condition of clients both from my interviews with service providers and from a broader observation of the state-of-the-art situation in public administration in general.

The short answer to the question is "yes." As has been demonstrated throughout this Element, workers provide clients with a broad range of resources that are not provided formally. Certainly, clients who receive such IFRs are better off with them than without them, and better off than clients who do not receive these resources, formally or informally. The provision of IFRs is closely related to welfare-state reforms, which have reduced public resources and altered the ability of citizens to receive many aspects of state support. In light of recent arguments about the importance of organizational embeddedness in increasing clients' well-being (Small & Gose, 2020), the significance and usefulness of IFRs received from frontline workers in this climate is unquestionable.

Specifically, workers' IFR provision increases the ability of people who belong to weakened populations to cope with various hardships, similar to the power of informal organizational resources found by Small (2006, 2009b). While Small's studies focused on the organizational level, the phenomenon described here emphasizes the crucial role of the individual worker's personal capital. In other words, it is not the "organization" that facilitates clients' well-being, but rather the informal practices of its workers, through which they directly provide their own resources to clients. This direct provision of personal resources in their interactions with clients makes the advantages of receiving these resources highly visible, allowing us to assume a direct link between resource provision and clients' increased well-being: they now have in their possession all the time, energy, knowledge, emotional encouragement, material goods, etc., that they received during their interaction with the frontline workers.

However, alongside the positive client outcomes of IFR provision, several other aspects of the phenomenon are likely to be less desirable. First, the receipt of personal resources, intended to enhance clients' well-being, might have an opposite effect in the long run: the mere fact that such provision is not routine, offered equally to all clients or based on clear criteria could create confusion, misunderstandings, and lack of trust in the system. For example, a client who receives an IFR from a certain worker might feel angry or frustrated if the same IFR is not provided the next time by the same worker or another worker. Furthermore, those clients who do not receive such personal resources might lose trust in the system after observing others who do. As IFRs are frequently provided when workers and clients have less formal, more personal relationships, the inability to create close relationships with workers might intensify feelings of exclusion among people who belong to weaker populations.

This leads to the second problematic aspect of IFR provision, which is the possible intensification of inequality, as such informal practices might enhance the well-being of those who receive these resources and reduce the well-being of those who do not. Broad literature demonstrates that frontline workers make discretionary decisions based on dominant common perceptions of morality about the worthiness and deservingness of clients (Brodkin, 2011; Harrits, 2019; Watkins-Hayes, 2011), strongly influenced by the current market-oriented disciplinary regime (Schram et al., 2009), according to which work commitment serves as the strongest moral indicator of character and as a rule for social inclusion or exclusion. Those who succeed in demonstrating efforts of being "hard workers" are perceived as "deserving" of collective support (Jilke & Tummers, 2018; van Oorschot, 2010), while those perceived as not showing willingness to take personal responsibility are considered "undeserving" (Lavee & Offer, 2012). It is quite possible that discretionary decisions about the provision of workers' personal resources are made according to similar worthiness criteria, thus harshly affecting the weakest clients who are not considered deserving of organizational support or of workers' informal support.

Beyond these problematic consequences for clients, there is a profound, far-reaching negative ramification, potentially influencing the entire operational processes of public service provision. We have seen that, when public resources are reduced, workers take it upon themselves to fill in for the widening service gap and provide personal resources to substitute for the withdrawing state. As a result, from a narrow, local perspective, clients/citizens are unlikely to recognize the full meaning of reduced state support. The state assumes that individual workers will act as a buffer against its citizens, as those who fill the public "hole" with their own capital. As suggested earlier, these personal resources may ease local hardships and allow a short-term increase in well-being. However, this anesthetizes the system, preventing full public acknowledgment of the meaning of lack of adequate public resources and services. Consequently, actions of public protests are avoided. While such consequences may be desirable for the state, personal resources, even when provided regularly by individual workers, cannot substitute for ongoing public support. Hence, at the bottom line, informal resources and services might intensify hardships and expand social inequalities.

7.2 The Broader Ramifications of IFR Provision for Public Administration

The picture presented in Section 7.1 reveals the contemporary nature of work in public administration as first and foremost characterized by a constrained environment shaped by scarcity of governmental and organizational resources. In such an environment, the discretionary element at the front line of policy work has become more significant in achieving policy outcomes (Brodkin, 2011), and public-sector workers are in fact coerced into using discretion to implement policy (Lavee & Strier, 2019). The provision of their personal resources has therefore become a main route to respond to client needs and compensate for an inadequate formal response.

When analyzing workers' rationales for providing their personal resources, we found that public-sector workers felt coerced to provide them. They also felt they have a broad responsibility for citizens, and, compared to other sectors, they seem to have less control over the personal, familial, and professional costs associated with IFR provision. Whether conceptualized as practices of "coerced discretion" (Lavee & Strier, 2019) or as compulsory OCB (Vigoda-Gadot, 2006), the provision of IFRs might have far-reaching consequences for both individual workers and public administration more generally. The consequences for individual workers have already been discussed (see Section 6); they include increased stress, intentions of leaving, and burnout – to name but a few. But the negative outcomes for public-sector organizations and the overall public administration are more subtle.

In terms of the costs for organizations, not only are exhausted workers characterized by higher turnover, but also they tend to provide poorer services. Under conditions of increased market pressures and higher competition even within public-sector organizations (Vigoda-Gadot, 2007), bad service is very bad for business. As for public administration more generally, workers who feel less in control, face multiple work constraints, and perceive their work as subjecting them to high costs are more likely to leave for other sectors. New workers are unlikely to be very enthusiastic about filling these vacated positions. As the public sector in many countries suffers from a shortage in workers, and the new generation of workers is more attracted to the nonprofit and private sectors (Ng, Gossett & Winter, 2016), the broad scope of IFR provision may definitely be one more factor leading to dwindling manpower and difficulties recruiting newcomers. In light of calls for expanded contemporary knowledge about individual workers' motivations to work in public services (Christensen, Paarlberg & Perry, 2017), insight yielded from the studies presented here might prompt some practical ideas for improving both service delivery and worker satisfaction.

It is important to state that the compulsory aspect of IFR provision and its negative ramifications, which are most prominent among public-sector workers, may also appear to a certain extent among workers in the nonprofit and private sectors. As was demonstrated, informal practices were often considered part of formal work for private-sector workers. Referring to compulsory OCB, Vigoda-Gadot (2006, p. 84) argued that blurred boundaries between the formal and the informal are often the result of external pressure from managers who are well aware of the organizational benefits of OCB, "exerting strong pressure on individuals to engage in unrecompensed extra-role work activities beyond their formal job definitions and creating a social atmosphere in which working extra hours beyond the formal work day with no formal compensation becomes the accepted norm" (2006:84). Therefore, private-sector workers may feel that, unless they are willing to engage in informal practices and provide personal resources to clients, their formal position in the organization will be jeopardized.

7.3 Gender Ramifications

Women tend to be overrepresented in the "caring professions," such as nursing, education, and social work (England, 2005), and constitute the vast majority of workers in the social services (US Bureau of Labor Statistics, 2021). Likewise, the vast majority of participants in the two studies reported here were women, as women form the majority of social service workers in Israel as well (Israel Central Bureau of Statistics, 2019). Feminist scholars have argued that the work in all these professions is based on perceptions of support, kindness, nurturing and empathy – "maternal" behaviors that are unrewarded, reflecting the assumption that care is a natural activity (Guy & Newman, 2004; Yang & Guy, 2014). As caring and sacrifice are assumed to be inherent to femininity, gender has always been a key aspect within worker–client interactions. Such behaviors are widely expected of women in organizations in general and of the majority-female staff of the social services in particular (Glinsner et al., 2019). Baines and Armstrong (2019) have argued that service delivery, including encounters with clients and their families, therefore reflects and reproduces traditional perceptions regarding gender relations and gender roles.

The phenomenon of IFR provision offers some important insights relevant to the broad literature on gender in public administration. Such provision of personal resources is performed under conditions of welfare and managerial reforms, which reduce public expenses and increase frontline workers' discretion, essentially transferring responsibility for social service provision from the state to the individual worker (Lavee et al., 2018). Further, such expectations of increased worker responsibility occurs alongside the ascription of increased importance to service provision in organizations. Because women are more sensitive to expectations of responsiveness to client needs than men (Potipiroon, Srisuthisa-ard & Faerman, 2019), the female worker's assumption of responsibility for and response to her clients' needs may lead her to offer a wide range of personal resources so as to ensure an adequate response. As people have a finite amount of physical and psychological resources, the more resources she invests in clients, the more likely she is to experience a deficiency of resources to invest in her nonwork domain.

These conclusions join recent arguments about the gender ramifications of the contemporary public administration environment. For example, in his work on street-level policy entrepreneurship, Cohen (2021) explained that, by shouldering activities of entrepreneurship, workers are actually engaged in off-duty activities, without formal recognition or compensation for their efforts. He argued that, as the majority of street-level workers are women, particularly those providing social services in such areas as welfare, health, and education, these activities have specific gendered consequences. Moreover, these extra-role activities can be framed along a continuum of compulsion to coercion, similar to other unpaid work that women take upon themselves (Baines, Cunningham & Shields, 2017). Therefore, the provision of IFRs, like policy entrepreneurship activities, might be the consequence of female workers' conformity to social role expectations (Riccucci, 2017) that they should be nurturing, patient, altruistic, and able to sense and respond to overall client needs (Baines & Armstrong, 2019; Guy & Newman, 2004). Drawing on the findings presented in this Element on the coerced aspect of IFR provision, particularly among public-sector workers, and the lack of control these workers have over the costs associated with informal practices, we can conclude that female frontline service providers are particularly vulnerable to the depletion of their own resources.

7.4 Some Preliminary Recommendations for Future Policy

In the Introduction to this Element, I underscored the large gap between the massive frequency of informal practices enacted by frontline workers in all sectors and the scarcity of scholarly evidence of this common phenomenon. I hypothesized that one of the main reasons for this is the will of certain actors to maintain the status quo. The state and its organizations avoid asking questions and therefore never receive some basic truths of how citizens ultimately receive adequate services despite the lack of adequate formal resources. Unfolding the broad phenomenon of IFR provision thus highlights the urgent need to adjust policy to citizens' needs, as well as to ease the constraints under which frontline workers provide services to clients.

Policymakers, practitioners, and scholars can draw on the findings presented here – namely, the personal resources that workers provide to clients – to learn about those resources that are missing the most and are essential to provide an adequate policy response to citizens. One example is the various aspects of instrumental informal services that healthcare teams (physicians, nurses, and other professionals and nonprofessionals) provide to clients in matters above and beyond their routine work (e.g., making appointments for clients in other facilities, helping them cut through red tape, and serving as a liaison with other social services). A major practical implementation emerging from this key finding could be the establishment in public hospitals and clinics of a supportive operation that supplements the medical-professional role of doctors and nurses. Indeed, the role of existing administrative staff is to provide support for various administrative matters, but the findings revealed that clients often need more comprehensive assistance, particularly as their encounters with health systems occur when they are in a highly vulnerable position.

Another example is the material resources provided by teachers. The public educational system cannot expect teachers to use their own resources in response to the variety of material shortages faced by the families of many of their students. An adequate policy would ensure that all schoolchildren have at least the basics that allow them to concentrate on their studies: school supplies, school uniforms (or adequate clothing and shoes), food for the entire school day, and money for transportation. This policy should focus on students more than their families. In other words, in addition to a social worker in charge of the family's overall welfare, a specific worker should be placed in schools to ensure that the individual student's basic needs are met, and not out of teachers' pockets.

These recommendations focus on the public sector, even though emotional, instrumental, and material aspects within all policy domains were broadly manifested by frontline workers in the nonprofit and the private sectors as well. This is because such changes are critical to public administration, whereas in the nonprofit and private sector, the institutional context is different, benefits and salaries are higher, and the workload is lower.

Learning from the findings presented in this Element could clearly benefit citizens who need assistance and have heretofore been receiving it randomly through the informal practices of (mainly) public-sector workers. Moreover, acknowledgment of the necessity of some of these services and their inclusion in formal organizational services would allow organizations to compensate workers for the resources they have become accustomed to providing out of their own capital. Such actions would reduce the current burnout that workers experience from providing both formal and informal resources. Moreover, reducing their workload and increasing the rewards of their work could make public-sector jobs much more attractive, facilitating the recruitment of new and eager workers to public administration.

References

Andersen, L. B. (2009). What determines the behaviour and performance of health professionals? Public service motivation, professional norms and/or economic incentives. *International Review of Administrative Sciences*, *75*(1), 79–97. http://doi.org/10.1177/0020852308099507.

Baarspul, H. C., & Wilderom, C. P. M. (2011). Do employees behave differently in public- vs private-sector organizations? *Public Management Review*, *13* (7), 967–1002. http://doi.org/10.1080/14719037.2011.589614.

Baines, D., & Armstrong, P. (2019). Non-job work/unpaid caring: Gendered industrial relations in long-term care. *Gender, Work & Organization*, *26*(7), 934–947. https://doi.org/10.1111/gwao.12293.

Baines, D., Cunningham, I., & Shields, J. (2017). Filling the gaps: Unpaid (and precarious) work in the nonprofit social services. *Critical Social Policy*, *37* (4), 625–645. http://doi.org/10.1177/0261018317693128.

Becker, H. S. (1996). The epistemology of qualitative research. In R. Jessor, A. Colby & R. Sweder (eds.), *Ethnography and human development: Context and meaning in social inquiry*, 27 (53–71). Chicago, IL: University of Chicago Press.

Benjamin, O. (2016). *Gendering Israel's outsourcing: The erasure of employees' caring skills*. New York: Springer.

Bergeron, D. M. (2007). The potential paradox of organizational citizenship behavior: Good citizens at what cost? *Academy of Management Review*, *32* (4), 1078–1095. http://doi.org/10.5465/amr.2007.26585791.

Bøgh Andersen, L., & Serritzlew, S. (2012). Does public service motivation affect the behavior of professionals? *International Journal of Public Administration*, *35*(1), 19–29. http://doi.org/10.1080/01900692.2011 .635277.

Bolino, M. C., & Grant, A. M. (2016). The bright side of being prosocial at work, and the dark side, too: A review and agenda for research on other-oriented motives, behavior, and impact in organizations. *Academy of Management Annals*, *10*(1), 599–670. http://doi.org/10.5465/19416520 .2016.1153260

Bolino, M. C., Klotz, A. C., Turnley, W. H., & Harvey, J. (2013). Exploring the dark side of organizational citizenship behavior. *Journal of Organizational Behavior*, *34*(4), 542–559. https://doi.org/10.1002/job.1847.

Bolino, M. C., & Turnley, W. H. (2005). The personal costs of citizenship behavior: The relationship between individual initiative and role overload, job stress, and work-family conflict. *Journal of Applied Psychology, 90*(4), 740–748. http://doi.org/10.1037/0021-9010.90.4.740.

Boyte, H. C. (2005). Reframing democracy: Governance, civic agency, and politics. *Public Administration Review, 65*(5), 536–546. https://doi.org/10.1111/j.1540-6210.2005.00481.x.

Bröckling, U. (2015). *The entrepreneurial self: Fabricating a new type of subject.* London: SAGE.

Brodkin, E. Z. (2006). Bureaucracy redux: Management reformism and the welfare state. *Journal of Public Administration Research and Theory, 17*(1), 1–17. http://doi.org/10.1093/jopart/muj019.

Brodkin, E. Z. (2011). Policy work: Street-level organizations under new managerialism. *Journal of Public Administration Research and Theory, 21* (suppl 2), i253–i277. http://doi.org/10.1093/jopart/muq093.

Bryson, J., Crosby, B., & Bloomberg, L. (2014). Public value governance: Moving beyond traditional public administration and the New Public Management. *Public Administration Review, 74*(4), 445–456. https://doi.org/10.1111/puar.12238.

Bryson, J., Crosby, B., & Bloomberg, L. (2015). *Public value and public administration.* Washington, DC: Georgetown University Press.

Burawoy, M. (1998). The Extended Case Method. *Sociological Theory, 16*(1), 4–33. https://doi.org/10.1111/0735-2751.00040.

Charmaz, K. (2014). *Constructing grounded theory.* London: SAGE.

Christensen, R. K., Moon, K.-K., & Whitford, A. B. (2021). Genetics and sector of employment. *International Public Management Journal, 24*(5), 585–595. http://doi.org/10.1080/10967494.2020.1802631.

Christensen, R. K., Paarlberg, L., & Perry, J. L. (2017). Public service motivation research: Lessons for practice. *Public Administration Review, 77*(4), 529–542. https://doi.org/10.1111/puar.12796.

Cohen, N. (2016). How culture affects street-level bureaucrats' bending the rules in the context of informal payments for health care: The Israeli case. *The American Review of Public Administration, 48*(2), 175–187. http://doi.org/10.1177/0275074016665919.

Cohen, N. (2021). *Policy entrepreneurship at the street level: Understanding the effect of the individual.* Cambridge: Cambridge University Press.

Cohen, N., Benish, A., & Shamriz-Ilouz, A. (2016). When the clients can choose: Dilemmas of street-level workers in choice-based social services. *Social Service Review, 90*(4), 620–646. http://doi.org/10.1086/689621.

Denhardt, J. V., & Denhardt, R. B. (2015). *The New Public Service: Serving, not steering.* New York: Routledge.

Denzin, N. K., & Lincoln, Y. S. (2008). *The landscape of qualitative research*, vol. 1. Thousand Oaks, CA: : SAGE.

Destler, K. N. (2016). A matter of trust: Street level bureaucrats, organizational climate and performance management reform. *Journal of Public Administration Research and Theory, 27*(3), 517–534. http://doi.org/10.1093/jopart/muw055.

Dörrenbächer, N. (2017). Europe at the frontline: Analysing street-level motivations for the use of European Union migration law. *Journal of European Public Policy, 24*(9), 1328–1347. http://doi.org/10.1080/13501763.2017.1314535.

Dubois, V. (2016). *The bureaucrat and the poor: Encounters in French welfare offices*. New York: Routledge.

Ebrahim, A., Battilana, J., & Mair, J. (2014). The governance of social enterprises: Mission drift and accountability challenges in hybrid organizations. *Research in Organizational Behavior, 34*, 81–100.

Eldor, L. (2017). Public service sector: The compassionate workplace – The effect of compassion and stress on employee engagement, burnout, and performance. *Journal of Public Administration Research and Theory, 28*(1), 86–103. http://doi.org/10.1093/jopart/mux028.

England, P. (2005). Gender inequality in labor markets: The role of motherhood and segregation. *Social Politics: International Studies in Gender, State & Society, 12*(2), 264–288. http://doi.org/10.1093/sp/jxi014.

Evans, T. (2012). Organisational rules and discretion in adult social work. *The British Journal of Social Work, 43*(4), 739–758. http://doi.org/10.1093/bjsw/bcs008.

Evans, T. (2016). *Professional discretion in welfare services: Beyond street-level bureaucracy*. London: Routledge.

Evans, T., & Hupe, P. (2020). *Discretion and the quest for controlled freedom*. New York: Springer.

Fossestøl, K., Breit, E., Andreassen, T. A., & Klemsdal, L. (2015). Managing institutional complexity in public sector reform: Hybridization in front-line service organizations. *Public Administration, 93*(2), 290–306. https://doi.org/10.1111/padm.12144.

Freidson, E. (2001). *Professionalism, the third logic: On the practice of knowledge*. Chicago, IL: University of Chicago Press.

Giauque, D., Ritz, A., Varone, F., & Anderfuhren-Biget, S. (2012). Resigned but satisfied: The negative impact of public service motivation and red tape on work satisfaction. *Public Administration, 90*(1), 175–193. https://doi.org/10.1111/j.1467-9299.2011.01953.x.

Glinsner, B., Sauer, B., Gaitsch, M., Penz, O., & Hofbauer, J. (2019). Doing gender in public services: Affective labour of employment agents. *Gender, Work & Organization, 26*(7), 983–999. https://doi.org/10.1111/gwao.12263.

Gofen, A. (2013). Mind the gap: Dimensions and influence of street-level divergence. *Journal of Public Administration Research and Theory, 24*(2), 473–493. http://doi.org/10.1093/jopart/mut037.

Guy, M. E., & Newman, M. A. (2004). Women's jobs, men's jobs: Sex segregation and emotional labor. *Public Administration Review, 64*(3), 289–298. https://doi.org/10.1111/j.1540-6210.2004.00373.x.

Hacker, J. S. (2019). *The great risk shift: The new economic insecurity and the decline of the American dream*: Oxford University Press.

Harrits, G. S. (2019). Stereotypes in context: How and when do street-level bureaucrats use class stereotypes? *Public Administration Review, 79*(1), 93–103. https://doi.org/10.1111/puar.12952.

Hartmann, J., & Khademian, A. M. (2010). Culture change refined and revitalized: The road show and guides for pragmatic action. *Public Administration Review, 70*(6), 845–856. https://doi.org/10.1111/j.1540-6210.2010.02216.x.

Harvey, D. (2007). *A brief history of neoliberalism*. Oxford: Oxford University Press.

He, P., Zhou, Q., Zhao, H., Jiang, C., & Wu, Y. J. (2020). Compulsory citizenship behavior and employee creativity: Creative self-efficacy as a mediator and negative affect as a moderator. *Frontiers in Psychology, 11*, 1640–1640. http://doi.org/10.3389/fpsyg.2020.01640.

Hsieh, C.-W. (2014). Burnout among public service workers: The role of emotional labor requirements and job resources. *Review of Public Personnel Administration, 34*(4), 379–402. http://doi.org/10.1177/0734371x 12460554.

Hupe, P., & Buffat, A. (2014). A public service gap: Capturing contexts in a comparative approach of street-level bureaucracy. *Public Management Review, 16*(4), 548–569. http://doi.org/10.1080/14719037.2013.854401.

Hupe, P., & Hill, M. (2007). Street-level bureacracy and public accountability. *Public Administration, 85*(2), 279–299. https://doi.org/10.1111/j.1467-9299 .2007.00650.x.

Hupe, P., & Krogt, T. v. d. (2013). Professionals dealing with pressures. In N. Mirko & S. Bram (eds.), *Professionals under pressure: The reconfiguration of professional work in changing public services* (pp. 55–72). Amsterdam: Amsterdam University Press.

Jilke, S., & Tummers, L. (2018). Which clients are deserving of help? A theoretical model and experimental test. *Journal of Public Administration Research and Theory, 28*(2), 226–238. http://doi.org/10.1093/jopart/muy002.

Koopman, J., Lanaj, K., & Scott, B. A. (2015). Integrating the bright and dark sides of OCB: A daily investigation of the benefits and costs of helping others. *Academy of Management Journal, 59*(2), 414–435. http://doi.org/10.5465/amj.2014.0262.

Kosar, K. R., & Schachter, H. L. (2011). Street level-bureaucracy: The dilemmas endure. [Street-level bureaucracy: Dilemmas of the individual in public services, Michael Lipsky]. *Public Administration Review, 71*(2), 299–302. www.jstor.org/stable/41061191.

Krøtel, S. M. L., & Villadsen, A. R. (2016). Employee turnover in hybrid organizations: The role of public sector socialization and organizational privateness. *Public Administration, 94*(1), 167–184. https://doi.org/10.1111/padm.12211.

Lam, C. F., & Mayer, D. M. (2014). When do employees speak up for their customers? A model of voice in a customer service context. *Personnel Psychology, 67*(3), 637–666. https://doi.org/10.1111/peps.12050.

Lavee, E. (2021). Who is in charge? The provision of informal personal resources at the street level. *Journal of Public Administration Research and Theory*, 31(1), 4–20.

Lavee, E., & Cohen, N. (2019). How street-level bureaucrats become policy entrepreneurs: The case of urban renewal. *Governance, 32*(3), 475–492. https://doi.org/10.1111/gove.12387.

Lavee, E., Cohen, N., & Nouman, H. (2018). Reinforcing public responsibility? Influences and practices in street-level bureaucrats' engagement in policy design. *Public Administration, 96*(2), 333–348. https://doi.org/10.1111/padm.12402.

Lavee, E., & Itzchakov, G. (2021). Good listening: A key element in establishing quality in qualitative research. *Qualitative research, 0*(0), 14687941211039402. http://doi.org/10.1177/14687941211039402

Lavee, E., & Offer, S. (2012). "If you sit and cry no one will help you": Understanding perceptions of worthiness and social support relations among low-income women under a neoliberal discourse. *The Sociological Quarterly, 53*(3), 374–393. http://doi.org/10.1111/j.1533-8525.2012.01240.x.

Lavee, E., & Pindek, S. (2020). The costs of customer service citizenship behaviors: A qualitative study. *Frontiers in Psychology, 11*(460). http://doi.org/10.3389/fpsyg.2020.00460.

Lavee, E., & Strier, R. (2018). Social workers' emotional labour with families in poverty: Neoliberal fatigue? *Child & Family Social Work, 23*(3), 504–512. https://doi.org/10.1111/cfs.12443.

Lavee, E., & Strier, R. (2019). Transferring emotional capital as coerced discretion: Street-level bureaucrats reconciling structural deficiencies. *Public Administration, 97*(4), 910–925. https://doi.org/10.1111/padm.12598.

Leete, L. (2000). Wage equity and employee motivation in nonprofit and for-profit organizations. *Journal of Economic Behavior & Organization, 43* (4), 423–446. https://doi.org/10.1016/S0167-2681(00)00129-3.

Lincoln, Y. S., & Denzin, N. K. (2003). *Turning points in qualitative research: Tying knots in a handkerchief,* vol. 2. Oxford: Rowman Altamira.

Lipsky, M. (2010 [1980]). *Street-level bureaucracy: Dilemmas of the individual in public service.* New York: Russell Sage Foundation.

Lyons, B. J., & Scott, B. A. (2012). Integrating social exchange and affective explanations for the receipt of help and harm: A social network approach. *Organizational Behavior and Human Decision Processes, 117*(1), 66–79. https://doi.org/10.1016/j.obhdp.2011.10.002.

Ma, E., & Qu, H. (2011). Social exchanges as motivators of hotel employees' organizational citizenship behavior: The proposition and application of a new three-dimensional framework. *International Journal of Hospitality Management, 30*(3), 680–688. https://doi.org/10.1016/j.ijhm.2010.12.003.

Maman, D., & Rosenhek, Z. (2011). *The Israeli central bank: Political economy, global logics and local actors.* New York: Routledge.

Maynard-Moody, S., & Musheno, M. (2000). State agent or citizen agent: Two narratives of discretion. *Journal of Public Administration Research and Theory, 10*(2), 329–358. http://doi.org/10.1093/oxfordjournals.jpart.a024272.

Maynard-Moody, S., & Musheno, M. (2003). *Cops, teachers, counselors: Stories from the front lines of public service.* Ann Arbor: University of Michigan Press.

Maynard-Moody, S., & Portillo, S. (2010). Street-level bureaucracy theory. In R. F. Durant (ed.), *The Oxford handbook of American bureaucracy* (pp. 252–277). Oxford: Oxford University Press.

Moynihan, D. P. (2008). *The dynamics of performance management: Constructing information and reform.* Washington, DC: Georgetown University Press.

Munyon, T. P., Hochwarter, W. A., Perrewé, P. L., & Ferris, G. R. (2009). Optimism and the nonlinear citizenship behavior: Job satisfaction relationship in three studies. *Journal of Management, 36*(6), 1505–1528. http://doi.org/10.1177/0149206309350085.

Ng, E. S. W., Gossett, C. W., & Winter, R. (2016). Millennials and public service renewal: Introduction on millennials and public service motivation (PSM). *Public Administration Quarterly, 40*(3), 412–428. www.jstor.org/stable/24772877.

Nielsen, T. M., Hrivnak, G. A., & Shaw, M. (2009). Organizational citizenship behavior and performance: A meta-analysis of group-level research. *Small Group Research, 40*(5), 555–577. http://doi.org/10.1177/1046496409339630.

Nieuwenhuis, R., & Maldonado, L. (2018). The triple bind of single-parent families: Resources, employment and policies to improve well-being. Bristol: Policy Press.

Nordhall, O., Knez, I., Saboonchi, F., & Willander, J. (2020). Teachers' personal and collective work-identity predicts exhaustion and work motivation: Mediating roles of psychological job demands and resources. *Frontiers in Psychology, 11*(1538). http://doi.org/10.3389/fpsyg.2020.01538.

Organ, D. W. (1988). Organizational citizenship behavior: The good soldier syndrome. Lexington, MA: Lexington Books/DC Heath and Com.

Osborne, S. P., ed. (2010). The new public governance? Emerging perspectives on the theory and practice. New York: Routledge.

Pache, A.-C., & Santos, F. (2012). Inside the hybrid organization: Selective coupling as a response to competing institutional logics. *Academy of Management Journal, 56*(4), 972–1001. http://doi.org/10.5465/amj.2011.0405.

Perry, J. L., & Wise, L. R. (1990). The motivational bases of public service. *Public Administration Review, 50,* 367–373.

Pollitt, C. (2010). Cuts and reforms – Public services as we move into a new era. *Society and Economy, 32*(1), 17–31. http://doi.org/10.1556/socec.32.2010.1.3.

Pollitt, C., & Bouckaert, G. (2017). Public management reform: A comparative analysis-into the age of austerity. Oxford: Oxford University Press.

Potipiroon, W., Srisuthisa-ard, A., & Faerman, S. (2019). Public service motivation and customer service behaviour: Testing the mediating role of emotional labour and the moderating role of gender. *Public Management Review, 21*(5), 650–668. http://doi.org/10.1080/14719037.2018.1500629.

Riccucci, N. M. (2017). Antecedents of public service motivation: The role of gender. *Perspectives on Public Management and Governance, 1*(2), 115–126. http://doi.org/10.1093/ppmgov/gvx010.

Roulston, K. (2010). Considering quality in qualitative interviewing. *Qualitative Research, 10*(2), 199–228. http://doi.org/10.1177/1468794109356739.

Schram, S. F., Soss, J., Fording, R. C., & Houser, L. (2009). Deciding to Discipline: Race, Choice, and Punishment at the Frontlines of Welfare Reform. *American sociological review, 74*(3), 398–422. http://doi.org/10.1177/000312240907400304.

Skelcher, C., & Ferlie, E. (2005). Public-private partnerships and hybridity. In E. Ferlie, L. E. Lynn Jr. & C. Pollitt (eds.), The Oxford Handbook of Public Management (pp. 347–370). Oxford: Oxford University Press.

Skelcher, C., & Smith, S. (2015). Theorizing Hybridity: Institutional logics, complex organizations, and actor identities: The case of nonprofits. *Public Administration, 93*(2), 433–448. https://doi.org/10.1111/padm.12105.

Small, M. L. (2006). Neighborhood institutions as resource brokers: Childcare centers, interorganizational ties, and resource access among the poor. *Social Problems, 53*(2), 274–292. http://doi.org/10.1525/sp.2006.53.2.274.

Small, M. L. (2009a). "How many cases do I need?": On science and the logic of case selection in field-based research. *Ethnography, 10*(1), 5–38. http://doi.org/10.1177/1466138108099586.

Small, M. L. (2009b). Unanticipated gains: Origins of network inequality in everyday life. Oxford: Oxford University Press.

Small, M. L., & Gose, L. (2020). How do low-income people form survival networks? Routine organizations as brokers. *The ANNALS of the American Academy of Political and Social Science, 689*(1), 89–109. http://doi.org/10.1177/0002716220915431.

Smith, S. R. (2010). Hybridization and nonprofit organizations: The governance challenge. *Policy and Society, 29*(3), 219–229. https://doi.org/10.1016/j.polsoc.2010.06.003.

Soss, J., Fording, R., & Schram, S. F. (2011). The organization of discipline: From Performance management to perversity and punishment. *Journal of Public Administration Research and Theory, 21*(suppl 2), i203–i232. http://doi.org/10.1093/jopart/muq095.

Statistics, I. C. B. o. (2019). *Statistical abstract of Israel.*

Statistics, U. S. B. o. L. (2021). Labor Force Statistics from the Current Population Survey. www.bls.gov/cps/tables.htm.

Steijn, B., & van der Voet, J. (2019). Relational job characteristics and job satisfaction of public sector employees: When prosocial motivation and red tape collide. *Public Administration, 97*(1), 64–80. https://doi.org/10.1111/padm.12352.

Thomann, E. (2015). Is output performance all about the resources? A fuzzy-set qualitative comparative analysis of street-level bureaucrats In Switzerland. *Public Administration, 93*(1), 177–194. https://doi.org/10.1111/padm.12130.

Thomann, E., Hupe, P., & Sager, F. (2018). Serving many masters: Public accountability in private policy implementation. *Governance, 31*(2), 299–319. https://doi.org/10.1111/gove.12297.

Thomann, E., van Engen, N., & Tummers, L. (2018). The necessity of discretion: A behavioral evaluation of bottom-up implementation theory. *Journal*

of Public Administration Research and Theory, *28*(4), 583–601. http://doi
.org/10.1093/jopart/muy024.

Tracy, S. J., & Hinrichs, M. M. (2017). Big tent criteria for qualitative quality. In
J. Matthes, C. Davis & R. Potter (eds.), *The international encyclopedia of
communication research methods* (pp. 1–10). Hoboken, NJ: Wiley-
Blackwell.

Tummers, L., & Bekkers, V. (2014). Policy implementation, street-level bureaucracy, and the importance of discretion. *Public Management Review*, *16*
(4), 527–547. http://doi.org/10.1080/14719037.2013.841978.

Tummers, L., Bekkers, V., Vink, E., & Musheno, M. (2015). coping during
public service delivery: A conceptualization and systematic review of the
literature. *Journal of Public Administration Research and Theory*, *25*(4),
1099–1126. http://doi.org/10.1093/jopart/muu056.

Tummers, L., Steijn, B., & Bekkers, V. (2012). Explaining the willingness of
public professionals to implement public policies: Content, context, and
personality characteristics. *Public Administration*, *90*(3), 716–736. https://
doi.org/10.1111/j.1467-9299.2011.02016.x.

van Oorschot, W. (2010). Public perceptions of the economic, moral, social and
migration consequences of the welfare state: An empirical analysis of welfare
state legitimacy. *Journal of European Social Policy*, *20*(1), 19–31. http://doi
.org/10.1177/0958928709352538.

Vigoda-Gadot, E. (2006). Compulsory citizenship behavior: Theorizing some
dark sides of the good soldier syndrome in organizations. *Journal for the
Theory of Social Behaviour*, *36*(1), 77–93.

Vigoda-Gadot, E. (2007). Redrawing the boundaries of OCB? An empirical
examination of compulsory extra-role behavior in the workplace. *Journal of
business and psychology*, *21*(3), 377–405. http://doi.org/10.1007/s10869-
006-9034-5.

Watkins-Hayes, C. (2011). Race, respect, and red tape: Inside the black box of
racially representative bureaucracies. *Journal of Public Administration
Research and Theory*, *21*(suppl_2), i233–i251. http://doi.org/10.1093/
jopart/muq096.

Whiting, S. W., Podsakoff, P. M., & Pierce, J. R. (2008). Effects of task
performance, helping, voice, and organizational loyalty on performance
appraisal ratings. *Journal of Applied Psychology*, *93*(1), 125–139. http://doi
.org/10.1037/0021-9010.93.1.125.

Yang, S.-B., & Guy, M. E. (2014). Gender effects on emotional labor in Seoul
Metropolitan Area. *Public Personnel Management*, *44*(1), 3–24. http://doi
.org/10.1177/0091026014550491.

Yildiz, B., & Elibol, E. (2021). Turnover intention linking compulsory citizen-ship behaviours to social loafing in nurses: A mediation analysis. *Journal of Nursing Management, 29*(4), 653–663. https://doi.org/10.1111/jonm.13200.

Zacka, B. (2018). *When the state meets the street*. Cambridge, MA: Harvard University Press.

Acknowledgment

The research presented in this Element was conducted with the generous support of the German-Israeli Foundation for scientific research & development.

Cambridge Elements ≡

Public and Nonprofit Administration

Andrew Whitford

University of Georgia

Andrew Whitford is Alexander M. Crenshaw Professor of Public Policy in the School of Public and International Affairs at the University of Georgia. His research centers on strategy and innovation in public policy and organization studies.

Robert Christensen

Brigham Young University

Robert Christensen is professor and George Romney Research Fellow in the Marriott School at Brigham Young University. His research focuses on prosocial and antisocial behaviors and attitudes in public and nonprofit organizations.

About the Series

The foundation of this series are cutting-edge contributions on emerging topics and definitive reviews of keystone topics in public and nonprofit administration, especially those that lack longer treatment in textbook or other formats. Among keystone topics of interest for scholars and practitioners of public and nonprofit administration, it covers public management, public budgeting and finance, nonprofit studies, and the interstitial space between the public and nonprofit sectors, along with theoretical and methodo-logical contributions, including quantitative, qualitative, and mixed-methods pieces.

The Public Management Research Association

The Public Management Research Association improves public governance by advancing research on public organizations, strengthening links among interdisciplinary scholars, and furthering professional and academic opportunities in public management.

Cambridge Elements ☰

Public and Nonprofit Administration

Elements in the Series

A full series listing is available at: www.cambridge.org/EPNP

Lightning Source UK Ltd.
Milton Keynes UK
UKHW020643180822
407492UK00013B/1319